From Napoleon's invasion of 1812 to the Wars of Liberation and beyond, seen from the common Russian soldier's perspective. This volume is composed of three accounts previously unavailable in English. Detailed annotations illuminate a seldom-understood army and nation during one of the pivotal episodes in European history.

Pamfil Nazarov was a state peasant from Tver who was conscripted in 1812 but, rather than head east to join the army in its campaign against Napoleon, he travelled to St. Petersburg and was selected for the Russian Imperial Guard. As a Jäger of the Finland Regiment he went on to witness such events as the Battle of Leipzig and the fall of Paris. Nazarov's memoirs also briefly describe the Russo-Turkish War of 1828, the Polish Uprising of 1830, and culminate in his voluntary induction into the monastic ranks of the Orthodox Church.

Ivan 'Menshoy' Ostroukhov similarly came from the peasantry of Tula and had prospects as a merchant before his household was chosen to produce a conscript. Also like Nazarov, he was inducted into the Guard, serving with the Uhlans as a choral singer in its reserve squadron. His autobiography ends prematurely, possibly due to the author's death.

Rafail Zotov, on the other hand, was a formally educated noble from St. Petersburg who could speak German and was familiar with astronomy and literature. He volunteered to serve as a junior officer in the militia when the French invaded. His preconceived notions of war and military service were challenged, and his abilities as a leader tested, by his experiences on the hard marches through the north to the battles of Polotsk and Berezina and on to the siege of Danzig in 1813.

Russia has a long and rich history and its self-identity is built on many episodes and myths, but none are so often dramatized, by Russians and Westerners alike, as Napoleon's invasion in 1812. Now for the first time the voice of the common Russian caught up in those continental events is available in the English language.

D1570936

Darrin Boland is an amateur historian and wargaming enthusiast from Hamilton, Ontario, Canada with a particular interest in Russian military history and the Napoleonic Wars in general. He has previously published translated primary documents through the Nafziger Collection.

Recollections from the Ranks

Three Russian Soldiers' Autobiographies from the Napoleonic Wars

Pamfil Nazarov, Ivan Ostroukhov, and Rafail Zotov

Translated and Annotated by Darrin Boland

Helion & Company Limited

Helion & Company Limited
26 Willow Road
Solihull
West Midlands
B91 1UE
England
Tel. 0121 705 3393
Fax 0121 711 4075
Email: info@helion.co.uk
Website: www.helion.co.uk
Twitter: @helionbooks
Visit our blog at http://blog.helion.co.uk/

Published by Helion & Company 2017
Designed and typeset by Mach 3 Solutions Ltd (www.mach3solutions.co.uk)
Cover designed by Paul Hewitt, Battlefield Design (www.battlefield-design.co.uk)
Printed by Lightning Source Ltd, Milton Keynes, Buckinghamshire

Translation, Foreword, and Notes © Darrin Boland 2017
Maps drawn by George Anderson © Helion & Company Limited 2017
Cover: 'The Veteran', lithograph by Pierre Jean Paul-Petit after Rudolf Żukowski. © Oleg
Polyakov

ISBN 978-1-912174-18-8

British Library Cataloguing-in-Publication Data.
A catalogue record for this book is available from the British Library.

For details of other military history titles published by Helion & Company Limited, contact
the above address, or visit our website: http://www.helion.co.uk

We always welcome receiving book proposals from prospective authors.

Contents

List of Plates and Maps

Translator's Foreword

This book collects three memoirs written by Russian participants of the Napoleonic Wars and translates them into English. These are the autobiographical works of Pamfil Nazarov, Ivan 'Menshoy' Ostroukhov, and Rafail Zotov.

What sets Nazarov's and Ostroukhov's writing apart from other memoirs of the era is that they were both written by conscripted state peasants, coming from a class which was overwhelmingly illiterate at the time and with less opportunity for social mobility – or even physical mobility – than the peasantry of most of Europe. It should be no surprise then to discover that both men were selected for the Imperial Guard, the fairer conditions of which undoubtedly contributed to their likelihood of survival and provided greater opportunities for personal enrichment. In the case of Nazarov, he did not learn to read and write until later in his life whereas Ostroukhov was tutored at a young age, but both men learned to read from monastic tutors and lacked formal education. Nazarov would later become a monk himself after his retirement from the military. Ostroukhov mentioned in passing during the opening chapters that he retired with the rank of captain, which would be an extraordinary progression for a commoner from the ranks in the Imperial Russian Army, but unfortunately his work is incomplete, so the story of his personal ascension into the petty nobility is left as a passing remark.

Conversely, the third man, Zotov, was a noble by birth who received a formal education and graduated with a diploma that granted him the lowest grade on the Table of Ranks: XIV. He first went into the civil service at the age of 16 and had only served for a year when Napoleon launched his invasion of the Russian Empire. When a general militia was raised, he volunteered and, by virtue of his diploma, was entitled to the lowest officer rank of ensign. Although from a significantly more privileged background and holding a higher position than the other two men, his memoir still tells the story of a teenager thrust into uniform during a national crisis and made to adapt nearly as roughly as the common soldiers in his unit. After his military service, Zotov became a playwright, novelist, and theatrical critic. Together, the three portray Russian society in general and the army in particular from the ground up and with personal testimony.

Pamfil Nazarov (1792-1839) came from the Tver Governorate, neighbour to Moscow, and was chosen for conscription when the French invasion had penetrated into the capital, but his recollections are notably apolitical. As the duty for providing a soldier fell on a household and not an individual, he was pressured by his own family to volunteer as his household's conscript in order to spare his other siblings. Two were married and the other was underage. This very same conflict appears as well in Ostroukhov's conscription. Instead of travelling east to join the main army, he went north-west to the Imperial capital of Saint Petersburg and was handpicked by the Emperor's brother, Constantine, for the Guard's Finland Regiment. He did not actually see his regiment until the truce in 1813 and from there went on to witness the battles of Dresden, Kulm, Leipzig, and ultimately Paris. He was wounded on multiple occasions, served through the Russo-Turkish War of 1828 and the Polish November Uprising of 1830 and was decorated with the soldier's cross of the Order of St. George, the medal of the Order of St. Anne, and all the appropriate campaign awards. He wrote his memoirs in 1839 under the assumed monastic name of Metrophanes, just a few months before his death, and his writings were not published until 1878 when they were discovered by the historical journal *Russian Antiquity* or *Tales of the Russian Past* (Русская Старина, *Russkaya Starina*).

Ivan Ostroukhov (1795-after 1873) was either from a poor merchant's family or an affluent peasant family with mercantile connections. His father died when he was young and he was hired out by his mother as a labourer to various persons in the province before his household was chosen by the recruitment levy and he was pressured into sacrificing himself to the army. On one occasion he was mistakenly recorded by the authorities by his nickname of 'Menshoy', meaning the younger or shorter – his other brother being called Ivan 'Bolshoy'. Then he was recorded mistakenly by his patronym 'syn Minayev' (Minayevich) as if it were his surname. His induction into the army was delayed and although he was called up to fulfil a levy from late in 1812, it was not until 1813 that he was shaved and sworn into service. Rather than be chosen for an infantry regiment like Nazarov, Ostroukhov was assigned to the Uhlan Regiment of the Guard and became a rider and trainer of remounts. He spent most of the Napoleonic Wars in a reserve squadron and never crossed the western frontier of the Empire. He never saw combat and his memoirs end in 1826 with the preparations for the coronation of Nicholas I. He became a non-commissioned officer after six years of service (four was the minimum), and wrote that he retired as a captain, but we are left to speculate on the circumstances. Being published in 1874 by *Russian Antiquity*, his writing concludes with 'to be continued' but in all the 175 issues of the journal, "Ivan Menshoy's Recollections" were never expanded on or concluded. Furthermore, the regimental history of the Uhlan Regiment of the Guard by Pavel Bobrovskiy contained an apparently exhaustive list of officers but no Ostroukhov, Minyev, or Menshoy appear in the relevant period. Perhaps his promotions into the officer corps came after a transfer to a different regiment or into the invalids. As the only other known Russian peasant-soldier contemporary with the Napoleonic Wars, his brief and sparse recollections are still an invaluable voice from a nation which had such a pronounced cultural divide between its state and nobility and the common people.

The writings of both Nazarov and Ostroukhov are brief, focused largely on personal experience with little thought for the broader political context and neither could speculate far on the strategic concerns of the battles which they witnessed. For both of them, the French invasion was not a galvanizing national awakening or a call to arms against a marauding enemy, it was a personal catastrophe that saw sons ripped from their homes, stripped and shaved in front of their neighbours, and then mourned pre-emptively as if they would never return, the term of service for a conscript being 25 years. Their writings also portray corruption and hypocrisy among their officers and the quick use of the cane to correct the men in the ranks. On the other hand, once they became acclimated to the soldier's life, they took pride in their uniform and relished every opportunity to see the Emperor and his family, which was more frequent for the Guard than other regiments might have enjoyed. They frequently use Church holidays and festivities instead of dates to provide context to the events in their lives, and idioms or clichés to explain phenomena they otherwise might not be able to articulate. They despised individuals when they were cruel, but they never questioned the social order or how that cruelty was enabled, and the promises of the French Revolution may well have never reached their ears. Their prose is quite far removed from the memoirs of Rafail Zotov (1795-1871).

Although a nobleman and an officer serving in a temporary militia which may as well be the polar opposite of the Imperial Guard, Zotov's service as a teenaged ensign, sent off to war after only a few weeks of drill, gave his writing the same naïve and uninitiated outlook as that of the two peasant-soldiers and he witnessed all of his new experiences from the company level. He did not ride on the march, but walked alongside the regular men. He laboured in their bivouacs to build their tents or impromptu huts of wicker and straw and faced the same bullets and artillery when manoeuvring on the battlefield. He conveys all of the enthusiasm for battle, and eagerness to be recognized for heroic deeds, of a teenaged boy raised on romantic fiction but he is also quick to remind the reader of how his experiences dispelled these myths. On the other hand, he gave in wholeheartedly to patriotic rhetoric and paints an image of a Russia completely united against France and liberating all of Europe along its way to rapturous applause. As a noble from St. Petersburg, the heart of the imperial bureaucracy and a city practically founded by servicemen and officers, his political perspective was highly idealistic and narrow in its portrayal of the nation. He frequently projects his own emotions onto his fellow officers or the common soldiers, and the effect is less convincing when paired with the writings of Nazarov and Ostroukhov. Zotov's prose is more literary and indulges in flights of passion and rhetorical asides with occasional references to novels, plays, and classical mythology which are completely absent in Nazarov and Ostroukhov. Still, as a participant of the Second Battle of Polotsk, a witness to the crossing of the Berezina and the terrible fate of the Grand Armée in the winter of 1812, and a participant in the Siege of Danzig for almost the whole of 1813, his memoirs contain the most numerous and detailed descriptions of combat and tactics of the three in this book. From bayonet charges to open-order skirmishing, from raiding parties on boats paddling over flooded plains to local village children digging up spent cannonballs to sell and fire back at their original owners, his memory was vivid and his pen was well honed by the time he wrote his memoirs. Despite only covering two years, they are longer and more detailed than the other two works combined. The typical bigotries against Poles and Jews appear briefly, but Zotov developed an uncharacteristic love for Germans at a time when the Russian officer corps largely fell into opposing Russian and German camps, where 'German' represented all foreign officers in general, but actual Germans in particular. He attributed it to the cordial welcome of many of the villages which hosted his unit and also to the amorous adventures he had in those territories. Conversely, Nazarov and Ostroukhov have nearly nothing to say about foreign nations, not even the Muslims of the Ottoman Empire. The similarity in scope of experience but radical differences in tone and political consciousness balance the three voices excellently.

In translating these memoirs, I have anglicised as much as possible wherever meaning would not be lost, but loanwords and idioms are left in as literally as possible, with explanations in footnotes. Some excessively long sentences have been broken up, and a few paragraphs as well, but the entirety of the content has not been abridged or censored (any more than in their original publications), nor rearranged for ease of reading or chronological order. For the most part, it was not necessary. The footnotes also provide context for major events, especially when they are mentioned in the text but are not dated, so that the reader can better understand where these memoirs fit into the larger historical narrative – this also includes providing dates for all the Orthodox holidays referenced.

Before 1918, Russia used a form of the Julian Calendar and dates from the 18th Century were 11 days behind the Gregorian Calendar adopted by most of Europe at the time. After 1800, dates lagged behind by 12 days.[1] All dates provided are given first in the original Russian dating according to the Julian calendar as it appeared in the original publications, and then followed in square brackets by the New Style dating relevant today. This pattern is continued even in the footnotes to prevent any confusion over which system is more relevant in a particular context – the Old Style is always first. Loanwords uncommon to English are always italicized, but are only explained once by a footnote. The names of members of the Imperial family or other European monarchs are anglicized, while other names are transliterated. Ecclesiastical names of Greek origin appearing in Nazarov's memoirs are spelled according to the Greek rather than their Russian forms. Polish place names are given for Congress Poland, especially for small towns and villages that would not be easily found by their Russian names, but the towns of

---

1   Семен Селешников, *История календаря и хронология* (Moscow: Наука, 1970), p.71. [Semyon Seleshnikov, *History of Calendars and Chronology* (Moscow: Science, 1970), p.71.]

East Prussia are given in German (as they appear in the memoirs), and those of the Lithuanian provinces of the Russian Empire are given in their Russian forms. The division of each memoir into chapters reproduces the chapters in the original publications and they vary dramatically in size. Nazarov's has seven short chapters and a postscript, Ostroukhov's has two halves, and Zotov's has three relatively long chapters. Zotov's own footnotes are reproduced and prefaced with 'Zotov's note': and enclosed in quotation marks.

The original concept for this book was to focus on only the two soldiers' memoirs but their combined length was too brief, so I sought out a similar text to counterbalance them and settled on Zotov's due to his rank and the unit in which he served. I had come across references to Nazarov and 'Minayev' in several secondary sources regarding the Russian Army in the Napoleonic Wars, both in English and Russian, with at most a sentence or two quoted, but I could not ever find them translated in their entirety into English. Having no other option, I sought out the original texts and produced a translation for myself. A project like this would not be possible without the endeavours of men such as Mikhail Semevskiy, the founder of the journal in which those two memoirs were first reproduced, and projects like Runivers which photograph and digitally preserve such books and journals and make them available from anywhere in the world. The proliferation of primary sources is vital in illuminating distant eras and nations, and this translation humbly seeks to contribute to that endeavour. I must also acknowledge George Nafziger who generously lent his time to help hone and publish this project, Oleg Polyakov for his work on the '1812' Internet Project and for giving permission to use artwork for the cover, and Nea Karvinen for her consultation on the Finnish language.

Darrin Boland
August, 2017

The Memoirs of the Soldier Pamfil Nazarov and Monk Metrophanes

I

The peasant Pamfil Nazarov, son of Nazar, was born on the 9th [20th] of February, 1792, in the village of Filimonova, Selikhovo township, Korcheva county, Tver province, on an economical estate,[1] and was christened on the 16th [27th] of that same month. I was very young when my father died, only five years old. Before coming of age, I did peasant's work in the summer and in the winter stoked fires. In the year of 1811, I learned how to forge nails and was faring rather well until April of 1812. Edicts on the conscript levies were sent out in that year. When I heard this news, I foresaw myself fated to military service and unable to escape it. I became badly depressed, fearing that the time had come I would have to leave my mother and brothers. The eldest was already married and had a son, for whom I had been named godfather; the second was also married; I, the third, was a bachelor; and the fourth brother in our family was not yet a man. The eldest raised us in place of our father, the second brother was very sick and frail, while I was a grown man and filled out, and the youngest was still small. That is why I often lamented my fate in private.

In September, our grandfather was ordered to attend a meeting. That day, I waited for him at home and could do nothing but lay down on the bench as if to sleep but cried bitter tears awaiting the terrible news. He returned home with our

---

1   Economic estates were properties formerly possessed by the Church and secularized through the Collegium of the Economy of the Synodal Board. In 1786, the collegium was abolished and the properties fell to the provincial treasuries, but the term remained in parlance. So-called 'economical peasants' were state peasants. И. Е. Андреевский, К. К. Арсеньев and Ф. Ф. Петрушевский, eds., *Энциклопедический Словарь Брокгауза и Ефрона*, 1st ed. (St. Petersburg: Ефрон, 1890), s.v. 'Экономические крестьяне.' [I. E. Andreyevskiy, K. K. Arsen'yev and F. F. Petrushevskiy, eds., *Brockhaus and Efron Encyclopedic Dictionary*, 1st ed. (St. Petersburg: Efron, 1890), s.v. 'Economical peasants.']

uncle Nikon Ivanovich and began to cry as he told the family, my mother and brothers, that our household was registered fourth.[2]

The family cried with him. I was silent, pretending to be sound asleep though my pillow was soaked in tears. Then I sat up and asked 'why are you crying?' Grandfather said again that our family was registered fourth. I spilled over with tears and ran to my fellow Feodor Ivanovich. Coming to his home, I saw him surrounded by his weeping family and on seeing me, he rushed to meet me, embracing me and bursting into tears as well. I said to him: 'well, brother, it's true that this is last time we'll stay in the homes of our parents!' His family was registered fifth. We went to my family's home and I ordered a troika of horses be harnessed in order to ride about and bid farewell in the village of Selikhovo and the hamlets of Dubrovka and Chublovo, where I stayed for several hours with a friend.

Returning home again, all of my family met me at the gate, teary-eyed, and made for a very sullen reception. In the house, there dropped to their knees my brothers, their wives and our old grandfather, who asked me to go into the army willingly for my brothers' sake, and my dear two-year-old godson, following his parents' example, fell and clung to my feet. And to these pleas I said nothing, for I knew that military service was my fate. Mother, ignoring her family and neighbours, told me plainly that 'for me, you're all equal'. Our godfather Pimen Ivanovich and my sister Avdotya Nazarovna advised mother to cast her vote for what was inevitable, but I told her that I was casting my lot in the Treasury Office and, dropping to her feet, thanked her for all she had so graciously done and provided for me.

After that, the sheriff came early in the morning with the orders to be in the village of Marino, where all the drafted were being sent. Having received such an order, we did not sleep all night. I asked my mother to stay home while my grandfather and brothers travelled with me. We gathered in the morning and received our elders' blessings, travelled with them down the road and said our mourning goodbyes to our relatives and neighbours with tears and pity. Then we parted from them.

In Tver, at the inn where we were staying, the elected elder arrived with orders to summon all of us to the offices of the provincial Treasury. After leaving the inn for the Treasury, my brothers and grandfather fell to my feet and begged again that

2   For recruitment, each county was divided into districts of 500 eligible males each, and a queue of households was drafted in each district based on how many able-bodied males there were, how economically stable the household was, and how recently they contributed to the levies. A rejection of a household's best candidate could see the authorities trying the next family on the list. An early placement in the queue made selection for contributing a recruit much more likely. The levy of 23 March [4 April] only called for 2 out of 500, but the levy of 30 November [12 December] increased to 8 out of 500 in order to replace heavy causalities from the campaign. *Полное Собрание Законов Российской Империи*, collection 1, vol. 30 (Moscow: II Отделение Собственное Его Императорского Величества Канцелярии, 1830), pp.248-251. [*Complete Collection of Laws of the Russian Empire*, collection 1, vol. 30 (Moscow: II Department of His Imperial Majesty's own Chancellery, 1830), pp.248-251.] No. 23,020.

I volunteer for my brothers. I teared up and left in haste for the Treasury offices. There I saw the other men being stripped and stood under the scale. Suddenly an old man came up to me and called me into the building where we were ordered to strip down to our shirts. We stood up against a mirror in the presence of the governor, who held the registry in his hands.[3] Going through the list, he called out our family and asked 'which of you is Pamfil?'

In a miserable voice, I answered: 'I am Pamfil'. Looking at me, he gave a motion with his head to signal a soldier to stand behind me, whom I did not notice until he took off my shirt. Needing to bare my chest seemed very strange to me, and I felt shy and ashamed when I saw a few hundred men around me all scrutinizing me like a convict.

The governor ordered him to bring me to the doctor who examined the inside of my mouth and looked over my whole body and then asked 'are you heathy?' I answered that I was and he relayed it back to the governor. He had me measured and my height came to two *arshins*, four *vershoks* and five eighths [162.8 cm]. The governor ordered 'forehead!' and I was shaved.[4] I got dressed again and was taken under guard. After being sorted, we took an oath and then were sent to our quarters.

I told my brother Mikhail Nazarych to immediately ride for home, some 60 *verstas* [64 km] from the city, to fetch our mother and the others. He left by evening and arrived at dawn, tethered the horse at the gate and quickly entered our parents' home, tearful, and gave a bow on my behalf as the new soldier. For my mother, this gesture was a terrible blow and she was beside herself for a short while. In the morning on the next day, they came to us during roll-call, after which the officer dismissed us to our quarters. At once I ran to my mother and she broke into tears as soon as she saw me, drenching herself. When we reached the barracks, I tried to convince her to stop crying and instead pray to God.

After staying in quarters for several days with our relations, an edict was sent calling for the recruits from the Tver province to be presented in Saint Petersburg via the postal road, so we were ordered to gather on the parade ground where the carts were prepared. The commander of our party, after taking roll-call, ordered us onto the carts. My family were overlooked and as I sat on the carts driving away, I could not forgive myself. It hurt me deeply that I could not say goodbye one last time and receive a blessing from my relations.

3   Luka Semyonovich Kologrivov was the governor of Tver from 12 [24] March, 1812 to 10 [22] March, 1813. Н. Ф. Самохвалов, ed., *Губернии Российской Империи* (Moscow: Russian Ministry of Internal Affairs, 2003), p.294. [N. F. Samokhvalov, ed., *Governorates of the Russian Empire* (Moscow: Russian Ministry of Internal Affairs, 2003), p.294.]

4   Shaving the front hemisphere of the head marked a man as an accepted conscript and made him identifiable should he desert. Shaving the back of the head and neck marked a man as rejected and spared him from being inducted twice. Richard Lister Venables, *Domestic Scenes in Russia* (London: John Murray, 1856), p.127.

We arrived in St. Petersburg on 3rd [15th] of October, 1812 at the Smolnyy Barracks and spent the night there. In the morning came an order to present us at an inspection at the Marble Palace to His Imperial Highness the Tsesarevich and Grand Prince Constantine Pavlovich. [5]Assembling us in a large hall and ordering us to open our rear two ranks, His Highness began to sort us into the Imperial Guard and the regular army. I was appointed to the army. But no sooner had I taken two steps than he watched me from behind, grabbed my shoulder and assigned me to the Finland Regiment of the Guard, for which I was sent to the Izmaylovo Barracks.

After serving for several days, I was sent with a few comrades to collect firewood, during which I met His Imperial Majesty Alexander I while walking along the bank of the Fontanka River, who asked me 'which regiment is yours and why are you out here?'

I replied timidly 'the *Leib*-Guard Finland Regiment. We came to collect firewood, Your Imperial Majesty!'

It was then ordered for us to learn the military drill. By the grace of God and the blessing of my kin, I realised very quickly that from the great pity of my family and the rigors of the army I had fallen ill, losing my mind at night on several occasions, which lasted for two weeks. During this time, my knapsack was robbed: my shirts, a cut of linen in which I had fifty [paper] assignation rubles, and so on.[6] I grieved the fact that I no longer wore the shirts of my family and was forced to buy from the marketplace.

After a few days, we were ordered to mount a guard in the city. A former non-commissioned officer in the guard detachment, having gotten drunk with a recruit at a tavern and entering the guard house after the drummer's mark of dawn, left me to stand watch for three additional hours for the sake of the recruit whom was with him, a command I obeyed willingly. Moreover, he forced me to train the recruit outside the prescribed times, to which I said 'I don't know anything and I can't teach except at the proper time'. For my refusal, he punched me bloody, yet I did not want to register a complaint and suffered in generous silence.

---

5   The title of Tsesarevich was held by the crown prince, next in line after the reigning Emperor of Russia. Grand Prince was a generic title held by members of the Imperial family. Alexander I had no children, so succession fell to his brothers. Constantine would later abdicate upon Alexander's death, resulting in the ascension of Nicholas Pavlovich to the throne. Леонид Шепелёв, *Титулы, Мундиры и Ордена Российской Империи* (Moscow: Центрполиграф, 2005), pp.402-411. [Leonid Shepelyov, *Titles, Uniforms and Orders of the Russian Empire* (Moscow: Tsentrpoligraf, 2005), pp.402-411.]

6   From the French '*assignat*', these rubles were paper notes with a nominal value in silver that was depreciated by excessive issuance and fragile market confidence. In 1801, the assignation ruble only exchanged for 66 kopecks and by 1817, it fell to 25 kopecks. Numerous attempts to buy them back with bullion and destroy them to control inflation were complicated by the continuous wars and their expenses. As payment, silver was always preferred. Geoffrey Hosking, *Russia: People and Empire* (Cambridge: Harvard University Press, 1997), p.106.

Grand Prince Constantine Pavlovich, Heir Apparent and Chief of the *Leib*-Guard Finland and Uhlan Regiments, among others. Aleksandr Orlovskiy, 1806, oil on canvas, Moscow, State Historical Museum.

The order came for us to join the regiment which was pursuing the French from Moscow.[7] His Imperial Highness wished to review us in parade, the month of February [1813] was spent marching past His Imperial Highness in columns of platoons. On the Semyonovskiy parade grounds there was held a thanksgiving service and we departed for Moscow Gate, where we young soldiers were accompanied by His Imperial Highness and many other people to bid us farewell. We were given carts for our muskets and knapsacks, but the rest of our kit was ours to carry.

7   The Finland Regiment departed St. Petersburg along with the Guard Jäger Regiment on the 2 [13] March, 1812 for Vilno (Vilnius) and joined the 1st Western Army by April. They had already fought at Borodino on 26 August [7 September] before Nazarov was conscripted and would see Tarutino on 6 [18] October shortly after his assignment to the regiment. Сергей Гулевич, *История Лейб-Гвардии Финляндского Полка*, Vol. 1 (St. Petersburg: Экономическая Типо-Литография, 1906), pp.175-230. [Sergey Gulevich, *History of the Leib-Guard Finland Regiment*, Vol. 1 (St. Petersburg: Economical Typo-Lithography, 1906), pp.175-230.]

We arrived in Prussia during a ceasefire,[8] and there I was assigned by the regimental commander to the 6th Jäger Company.[9] We were given musket training with targets and live ammunition, but my musket misfired and the captain ordered a note be made for the failure of my musket. After training was finished, I was flogged twice with a stick before the company, [once bare-chested and] once with my uniform on but without my equipment.

II

In July of 1813 came the order to give a real battle to the enemy, driving us through Silesia, Bohemia and Saxony to the city of Dresden, at which the enemy began a battle which saw two days of cannon fire, but heavy rain put a damper on musketry.[10] The army was held relentlessly in one place and suffered from a lack of provisions and were discontent from being drenched. We began to bombard them with explosives which lit up the city and then His Imperial Majesty ordered the Guard Corps to retreat along two roads to the city of Teplitz – the First Division taking the large highway and our Second Division travelling by a rougher country road. This was hard for us, since we were being pursued hastily by the enemy and all around us were forests and swamps. Our artillery and cavalry drove us off the road and forced us to walk through the swamp and deadwood, which was miserable going. We began our retreat from the city at 9 at night and continued until 8 in the morning.

We came to a hamlet which was no more than ten homes, beside which we encamped in the field to boil a soup, but before we could settle down, an enemy shot rang out and killed a drummer from the *Leib*-Grenadier Regiment.[11] The commander immediately ordered us to gear up and resume the retreat without delay. We continued until midnight and many of us had lost footwear, I being one of them. This day was for our army very tragic due to the shortages of food, footwear, and the poor weather. As soon as we emerged from the forest onto a field, we saw Emperor Alexander I passing us with the commander-in-chief Barclay

---

8   The Truce of Pläswitz between France and the Allies was accepted on 23 May [4 June], 1813 and lasted until 31 July [12 August], upon which Austria declared war on France and joined the alliance. A. W. Ward, G. W. Prothero and Stanley Leathes (eds.), *Cambridge Modern History*, Vol. 9 (Cambridge: University Press, 1906), pp.520-522.

9   From 1807 to 1815, the Finland Regiment was commanded by Maksim Konstantinovich Kryshanovskiy. He was a colonel during the 1812 campaign, but was promoted to major general on 15 [27] September, 1813. Gulevich, *Leib-Guard Finland Regiment*, Vol.1, pp.112-360.

10 The Battle of Dresden spanned 14-15 [26-27] August, 1813. Gulevich, *Leib-Guard Finland Regiment*, Vol.1, pp.296-7.

11 The Leib-Grenadier Regiment was inducted into the Guard with Junior Guard status on 13 [25] April, 1813, along with the Pavlovsk Grenadier Regiment, and was officially renamed the *Leib*-Guard Grenadier Regiment. *Complete Collection of Laws*, collection 1, Vol.32, pp. 555-556. No. 25,470a.

Emperor Alexander I of Russia (Reigned 1801-1825). François Gérard, 1817, oil on canvas, St. Petersburg, State Hermitage Museum.

de Tolly who was pointing to the soldiers marching barefoot. On seeing this, the Emperor wept and drew a white handkerchief from his pocket to dry his eyes. I then wept when I saw him so moved. When we reached the Saxon border, we repelled the enemy and an army corps relieved us. We were ordered to join the First Guard Division which was in the city of Teplitz.

We did not have time to learn that the First Division was already engaged in a battle and we had to hurry as quickly as possible to come to their aid. When the enemy saw us come to reinforce, they began to withdraw. His Highness attacked with his cavalry, crossed the road at Kulm, and captured the baggage train and many infantrymen.[12] The [regular] army corps had been ordered to pursue and our columns were ordered to hold our position where we stood. His Majesty Alexander I rode past us with his whole retinue to examine the bodies of the fallen and congratulate us on our victory. When his inspection was complete, he rode to quarters in the city of Teplitz, to which we also retired.

In the morning, the order was given through the whole Guard Corps to perform a parade for a thanksgiving service, which concluded with firing cannons and muskets in the presence of the Sovereign. Since the town had hot springs, the Sovereign paid a small amount so that the Guard Corps could bathe without prohibition and I was granted the luxury of being one of them. That same day it was ordered to bury the dead, and when the French supply train was divided, I was lucky enough to get a pair of shoes and gaiters. At that time, we lacked provisions, so the army was fed on potatoes and fruits.

After staying there for several days, we were ordered to head for the city of Leipzig, where our army had already fought for a day before our arrival.[13] When we arrived, we could see locations of both our whole army and the French. His Highness rode up to us and ordered us to load our muskets and enter the battle. On the approach, my greatcoat was repeatedly shot through and I was wounded by a bullet in the right thigh with damage to a vein from which blood began to flow, which felt warm like I was being doused in hot water. I immediately fell out and retreated – not many did the same – and became ill. I fell face down on the ground and had lain there for a length of time I cannot remember. A wounded NCO from our company approached me and, recognizing me, hauled me up. He asked me: 'can you walk at all?' I said that I could for a little while and he led the way. It was

12 The Battle of Kulm was fought on 17-18 [29-30] August, 1813. The baggage and infantry seized may refer to General Vandamme's corps, which at Kulm was badly beaten and captured along with its commander. Gulevich, *Leib-Guard Finland Regiment*, Vol.1, pp.300-301.

13 The Battle of Leipzig spanned the 4-7 [16-19] October, 1813. It was the largest battle of the period and was dubbed the 'Battle of the Nations' for all the states present and the scale of the fighting. The Finland Regiment had fought on the first day but the 2nd Battalion under Colonel Pyotr Sergeyevich Ushakov, to which Nazarov's company belonged, was in reserve. Perhaps his company arrived late or he confused the context of their absence from the initial fighting. For all the battle, the regiment fought in and around the village of Güldengossa. Gulevich, *Leib-Guard Finland Regiment*, Vol.1, pp.303-325.

still dangerous as cannon balls flew past us, so he left me and I gradually reached a village, which was not more than two *versta*s [2.14 km] away, and in which I found regimental banners, wagons, musicians and doctors bandaging the wounded. My wound was dressed there on the 4th [16th] of October, 1813.

Late at night, I set out down a large road to an unknown destination and came along a fire around which sat a Prussian and a wounded soldier from our company, who shared two pickled cucumbers with me. They were a wonderful treat, very dear to me, and helped to shore up my strength. Removing my pack, I lay by the fire and slept until 6 in the morning, waking up to find myself in a large pool of blood flowing from my wound. Binding my wound again and putting on my pack and cross belts, I set out down the road while leaning on my musket as a crutch.

Arriving at the city of Plauen in Saxony, I found the whole city full of the wounded, even in the homes, and there was no place left to rest and recover. For that reason we were sent to a cemetery at a Catholic church which was already brimming with nearly 400 wounded men. That place became my residence on the 16th [28th] of October. German doctors, barber-surgeons, and attendants were constantly among the wounded. In the morning, I was given two crutches which I used to go to get my wound dressed by a doctor. When he saw that my wound was festering since it had not been dressed in thirteen days, he took a needle as thick as a chicken's feather and as long as 5 *vershok*s [22.23 cm] and threaded it into my dressing with an ointment. The pain was so excruciating it was impossible to tolerate. Imagine being stuck with a needle in a deadly wound with a fresh tourniquet, which was a torment for me every day because the dressing needed to be changed and the wound cleaned each morning and evening for several days.

When my wound fully recovered, I still could not walk without crutches as my leg would cramp up and I could not flex it, but my comrades started to laugh at me as though I was faking being unable to walk, and would repeat many hurtful words to me. I wanted to prove to them I was being honest so in their sight I struck my leg on the ground and tore the tendons and renewed my wound even more painfully than the first time I was shot. For this, I was forced to be laid up and be treated again for six weeks in the hospital, during which the new year of 1814 began, and by then my right leg was restored but had become half a *vershok* [2.22 cm] shorter than the left.

Remaining in quarters for a few days, I was assigned to a detachment which came to the army from several hospitals and received boots and from the commandant. We set out again in the morning. I had travelled no further than four *versta*s [4.27 km] before severe aches set in due to a tumour in my leg from my old wound and I could not continue farther. An officer immediately ordered me put on a wagon and so I rode for several days into Bavaria and was again admitted into a hospital. My boots were removed and I was treated for a while. I was again discharged and returned to my quarters, from which shortly after I was again sent to join the army without crutches, limping only slightly, and my treasury-issued boots were returned to me.

We reached the city of Bautzen, where there was a serious battle on the 9th and 10th [21th and 22th] of March.[14] We drove the enemy from there straight to Paris without a delay on the 19th [31st] of March, 1814, in which our regiment was ordered to join the fight. But since the Cossack that was given our orders to deliver could not find us, a Prussian Guard regiment was sent in our place, which was almost completely shattered, and we had already headed out to aid the meagre collection of remaining soldiers.[15] Seeing such a miserable disgrace, we were stupefied with fear and did not know what to do, but with the aid of God and with a blessing from a priest's cross, we entered the battle.

As soon as we began however, we saw that the city gates opened and an ambassador left the fortress with documents and the keys to the city, announcing that the city surrendered to us. The general in command of the detachment received the keys and papers and made a signal, removed his hat and threw it up in the air. His senior adjutant standing nearby cried '*ura!*'[16] which we repeated several times. After that, we were ordered to remain at that outpost until morning and during that evening we prepared for the parade that would enter Paris at 6 in the morning.

The next day, His Imperial Majesty Alexander I, the Austrian Emperor,[17] the King of Prussia,[18] and the commanders-in-chief all arrived at our outpost.[19] They consulted together for a few minutes on how to enter the city. A Cossack squadron was ordered to ride ahead, behind them was the Emperor Alexander I, on his right side was the Emperor of Austria and on his left the King of Prussia with

14   The Battle of Bautzen was fought on 8-9 [20-21] May, 1813 in Saxony, not at all a ten-day march from Paris. Nazarov may have meant to refer to Arcis-sur-Aube, which saw an engagement on 8-9 [20-21] March, 1814. Gulevich, *Leib-Guard Finland Regiment*, Vol.1, pp.287-288; Ward et al., *Cambridge Modern History*, Vol.9, pp.552-553.

15   On 18 [30] March, 1814, a Prussian column under Lt. Colonel von Block containing the Fusilier Battalion of the 1st Guard Regiment and the 1st Battalion of the 2nd Guard Regiment advanced into the village of Pantin and became surrounded by French artillery and sharpshooters on three sides, losing most of its strength and retreating in disorder. Otto von Lüdinghausen genannt Wolff, *Geschichte des Königlich Preußischen 2. Garde-Regiments zu Fuß, 1813-1882* (Berlin: E. S. Mittler und Sonn, 1882), pp.39-45. [Otto von Lüdinghausen known as Wolff, *History of the Royal Prussian 2nd Guard Regiment of Foot, 1813-1882* (Berlin: E. S. Mittler and Son, 1882), pp.39-45.]

16   'Ypa' – a traditional Russian war cry and cheer, equivalent to the English 'hooray', German 'hurrah', etc. The etymology is uncertain but may come for the Tatar 'Yp' (ur') meaning 'strike; hit; blow'. It was still used in the world wars of the 20th Century and can be heard today during Russia's Victory Day celebrations. Andreyevskiy et al., *Brockhaus and Efron Dictionary*, s.v. 'Ypa.' [Andreyevskiy et al., *Brockhaus and Efron Dictionary*, s.v. 'Ura.']

17   Francis II and I, Holy Roman Emperor from 1792 to 1806 and Emperor of Austria from 1804 to 1835.

18   Frederick William III, King of Prussia from 1797 to 1840.

19   The Field Marshals Prince Carl Phillip zu Schwarzenberg from Austria, Michael Barclay de Tolly from Russia, and Gebhard von Blücher from Prussia and were the principal commanders during the Battle of Paris. Александр Михайловский-Данилевский, *Описание Похода во Францию в 1814 году*, Vol.2 (St. Petersburg: Типография Департамента Внешней Торговли, 1836), pp.252-311. [Aleksandr Mikhaylovskiy-Danilevskiy, *Description of the Campaign in France in 1814*, Vol. 2 (St Petersburg: Press of the Department of Foreign Trade, 1836), pp.252-311.]

Francis II of the Holy Roman Empire and Francis I of Austria (Reigned 1792-1804 and 1804-1835). Josef Kreitzinger, 1820, oil on canvas, Vienna, Museum of Military History.

Constantine Pavlovich. A few paces behind them were the generals, the Retinue and Convoy. Then marched the Preobrazhenskiy Regiment, the Austrian Guard's First Regiment,[20]and after them the Prussian Guard's First Regiment. In that order all three units marched in turn, followed by the regular army forces. The procession through Paris lasted from 8 in the morning until 9 in the evening. The entrance through Paris was very festive and all along the avenues we marched, several thousand people cried '*Vive Alexandre! Vive l'armée russe!*'[21] Such cries were almost palpable for us and filled us with joy, and the people flocked so to watch us that there were neither empty windows, nor rooftops, nor any structure without jubilant and curious spectators.

---

20 Austria had no Guard in the 1813-14 campaign or the Battle of Paris. The Austrians' Grenadier Brigade did participate in the battle and victory parade, however. Von Lüdinghausen's *History of the Royal Prussian 2nd Guard Regiment of Foot* and Mikhaylovskiy-Danilevskiy's *Description of the Campaign in France* both agree on a different order for the parade: the Prussian Guard's cavalry; the Russian Guard's Light Cavalry Division and a complement of over a thousand generals and officers; the Austrian Grenadier Brigade; the Russian Grenadier Corps; the Russian Second Guard Infantry Division, which contained the Finland Regiment; the Prussian Guard Infantry Brigade; the First Russian Guard Infantry Division, which contained the Preobrazhenskiy Regiment; the three Russian Cuirassier Divisions; and lastly a large combined artillery train. Mikhaylovskiy-Danilevskiy, *Description of the Campaign in France*, pp.310-311.; Von Lüdinghausen, *History of the 2nd Guard Regiment*, p.59.

21 French: 'Long live Alexander! Long live the Russian Army!'

F. de Maleque, The Entrance of the Allied Forces in Paris, 19 [31] March, 1814. 1815, oil on canvas, Moscow, A. S. Pushkin State Museum.

After passing through Paris, we stood in a field until 4 in the morning and then were ordered to retire to a Parisian barracks while the army corps pursued the enemy to the sea.[22] The occupation of Paris was not favourable for us: constant parades, drills and guard mountings. A few days later, the Grand Princes Nicholas and Michael Pavlovich deigned to visit the outpost at which the Izmaylovskiy Regiment of the Guard was stationed. Welcomed by the regiments, the Grand Princes said 'oh, you Russian eagles, how far you've flown!' This warmed our hearts and truly we had flown across twelve nations like eagles. In all, we spent two months and six days in Paris.

Receiving the order to return to the Russian frontier, the First Division set out straight to the Baltic Sea,[23] where ships were prepared for them to sail to St. Petersburg, and the Second Division marched to Berlin, the Prussian capital, in

22 The Finland Regiment was quartered in the École Militaire, and the field Nazarov mentioned may have been the adjacent Champ de Mars. Gulevich, *Leib-Guard Finland Regiment*, Vol 1, pp.337-342.

23 The Preobrazhenskiy Regiment marched to Cherbourg and boarded ships, landed in England for five days, and then reached Kronstadt and Oranienbaum by 18 [30] July, 1814. The rest of the First Guard Division presumably also headed to the English Channel from Paris and not to the Baltic Sea. С. Долгов and А. Афанасьев, eds., *История Лейб-Гвардии Преображенского полка. 1683-1883* Vol. 3, Part 1 (St. Petersburg: Типография И. Н. Скороходова, 1888), pp.132-133. [S. Dolgov and A. Afanas'yev, eds.,

King Frederick William III of Prussia (Reigned 1797-1840). Ernster Gebauer, 1820, oil on canvas, Wroclaw, Poland, Municipal Museum.

which we joined the Prussian King and his Guard. Entering the city in parade, we passed by the palace through the square where His Royal Majesty was in attendance and then settled into barracks and a few private homes in the city. Those hosting us were very pleased with our company.

That evening, the order was given to be ready in the morning for a meal with His Royal Majesty and the whole Guard Division, and our regiment was on the square opposite the palace where the tables were being prepared with food and drink. A non-commissioned officer from His Majesty's company, as per the itinerary, brought a glass of vodka to the King, for which he received a gold *chervonets* as soon as the King took the glass from him.[24] His Majesty then congratulated us on our victory and we shouted '*ura!*' He gave us permission to eat and then mounted

History of the Leib-Guard Preobrazhenskiy Regiment, 1683-1883, Vol. 3, Part 1 (St. Petersburg: Press of I. N. Skorokhodov, 1888), pp.132-133.]

24 *Chervonets* referred to coins minted in gold, which encompassed Russia's five- and ten-ruble coins, the latter also being known as an 'imperial'. The Prussian soldier was probably being rewarded in Fredericks d'Or however. Andreyevskiy et al., *Brockhaus and Efron Dictionary*, s.v. 'червонец.'; Ibid., s.v. 'империал.'; *Complete Collection of Laws*, collection 1, vol. 16, 691-692. No. 12,116. [Andreyevskiy et al., *Brockhaus and Efron Dictionary*, s.v. 'chervonets.'; Ibid., s.v. 'imperial.'; *Complete Collection of Laws*, collection 1, vol. 16, pp.691-692. No. 12,116.]

his horse and rode around the other regiments. After the meal was over, we started to fraternize with the Prussian regiments and the civilian audience until evening, and then retired to our quarters.

On the fourth day, we left for the city of Lübeck on the shore of the Baltic Sea, where thirteen Russian ships were prepared. We boarded them and departed. We sailed safely for several days when suddenly a large storm rose up and smashed the masts on the ship *The Myrrhbearer*,[25] which I was aboard. Fearing such a storm, we desperately dropped anchor and fired a signal shot from a cannon, hoisted the colours, and the other twelve ships came to our aid. After several hours, we had our masts repaired and set sail again. The storm intensified day after day, however, and our ships were continually knocked about. We were deprived of food for several days and became ill, though no one perished.

Approaching the city of Kronstadt, we saw that they had hoisted their flag and greeted us with a salute of cannon shots. We returned the salute and after arriving, sailed to the coast, to the city of Oranienbaum, six *versta*s [6.4 km] across the sea, where we were quartered close by. In the morning, we marched for St. Petersburg and on the fourth day we entered the city through a newly erected triumphal arch,[26] on which was inscribed the names of the regiments of the Guard. Upon entering, the Emperor, his August Family, and many burghers greeted us and we passed them by platoons in parade. Then we retired to our barracks. When we arrived, we were awarded each with a silver ruble and a bread roll, but severe exercises continued all through the winter. When spring came, the enemy again made war and we were ordered to go on the march again, reaching Riga. We stayed there until autumn, but as it is known, the enemy was defeated a second time and we returned to Russia.[27]

---

25 The Finland Regiment of the Guard boarded three 74-gun ships of the line on 17 [29] August, 1814. They were named 'Нептунус' (*Neptunus*), 'Мироносец' (*Mironosets*) and 'Память святого Евстафия' (*Pamyat' svyatogo Evstafiya*), literally 'Neptune', 'Myrrhbearer' and 'St. Eustice's Day'. Gulevich, *Leib-Guard Finland Regiment*, Vol.1, pp.344-345; *Список Русских Военных Судов с 1668 по 1860 год* (St. Petersburg: Типография Морского Министерва, 1872), pp. 52-55. [*A List of Russian Military Vessels from 1668 to 1860* (St. Petersburg: Press of the Naval Ministry, 1872), pp. 52-55.]

26 The original Narva Triumphal Gate was built of wood and plaster in 1814 to greet the army returning to the capital and was later replaced by a permanent stone arch which still stands today. The Finland Regiment passed through it and entered the city on 5 [17] September, 1814. Gulevich, *Leib-Guard Finland Regiment*, Vol.1, p.345; 'Нарвские Триумфальные ворота, памятник,' *Энциклопедия Санкт-Петербурга*, accessed July 28, 2016. ['Narva Triumphal gate, monument,' *Encyclopedia of Saint-Petersburg*, http://encspb.ru/object/2805471522?lc=ru., accessed July 28, 2016.]

27 The Hundred Days or the War of the Seventh Coalition effectively lasted from 8 [20] March, 1815, when Napoleon returned to Paris, to 26 June [8 July], when Louis XVIII retook the throne in a Second Restoration. Ward et al., *Cambridge Modern History*, Vol. 9, pp.616-645.

III

In 1816, in the month of September, I began to learn how to read and write and by Christmas I could already read the Book of Psalms and write correspondence. Many of my comrades, seeing me succeed so quickly, wanted to learn for themselves and I became their teacher, especially to Yegor Gavrilovich, who is now [in 1839] a monk at Valaam. I divided my free time thus: in the afternoon until evening I practiced writing and in the evening I read and began the first lessons of arithmetic, among other things.

On the 9th [21th] of February, 1821, I was granted leave until the 1st [13th] of May to visit my family. While living at home, I received a letter from a comrade that informed me the army began to march toward Turkey.[28] Returning to St. Petersburg on the 4th [16th] of May, I set off on the march on the 1st [13th] of June and joined the regiment in the city of Vilno. Billeted there, we remained for several months before returning to St. Petersburg in September of 1822.

On the 7th [19th] of November, 1824, there was a terrible flood in St. Petersburg which began at 8 in the morning and began to drain in the evening, the streets drying completely by midnight. The water had risen by two and a half *arshins* [177.8 cm].[29]

In November of 1825, the life of Emperor Alexander I came to an end in Taganrog and we chanted the Memory Eternal in honour of his valour! We also swore an oath to Emperor Nicholas I, during which terrible bloodshed erupted where I was.[30]

In March of 1826, we received medals for the French War and the capture of Paris with a portrait of His Imperial Majesty Alexander I and a radiant All-Seeing Eye, hung on a Georgian ribbon, while the reverse was embossed 'For the Capture

---

28 The mobilization of the army in 1821 was dubbed the 'Italian Campaign', as it came amid tensions at the Congress of Laibach regarding the Italian Uprisings of the previous year. However, the Greek Uprising against the Ottomans also broke out in 1821, and may have been a source of confusion for the soldiery. Gulevich, *Leib-Guard Finland Regiment*, Vol. 1, pp.446-449.; Ward et al, *Cambridge Modern History*, Vol. 10, pp.178-189.

29 Samuil Aller's *Description of the Flood in St. Petersburg on 7 November, 1824* reported water as high as 16 feet [487.7 cm] on Vasilevskiy Island, especially at the Galley Harbour on the western shore. Coincidentally, the Leib-Guard Finland Regiment's barracks were on Vasilevskiy. Самуил Аллер, *Описание Наводнения, бывшего в Санкт-Петербурге 7 числа ноября 1824 года*, (St. Petersburg: Типография Департамента Народного Просвещения, 1826), p.9. [Samuil Aller, *Description of the Flooding formerly in St. Petersburg on the 7th November 1824*, (St. Petersburg: Press of the Department of Public Education, 1826), p.9.]; Gulevich, *Leib-Guard Finland Regiment*, Vol. 1, pp.453-458.

30 The Decembrist Revolt broke out on 14 [26] December, 1825 in Peter's Square (now Senate Square) in St. Petersburg. On that day, the 2nd Battalion of the Guard Finland Regiment, containing Nazarov, were posted on guard duty in front of the Winter Palace, the Admiralty, Peter's Square itself, and various other positions around the city. He may have witnessed the violence first hand or may have only heard it from a distance. Gulevich, *Leib-Guard Finland Regiment*, Vol. 2, pp.1-22.

Commemorative Medal for the Patriotic War of 1812. Victory commemoration for participants. Plain silver. Light-blue ribbon. Reverse paraphrases Psalm 113:9 (115:1) 'Not to us, O Lord, not to us, but in your name…'. Viskovatov, *Historical Description of the Dress and Armament of the Russian Army* (St. Petersburg: Military Press, 1860), Vol.18, Plate 2580.

of the City of Paris, 19th [31st] March, 1814'.[31] On receiving these medals, we were sent to Moscow for the coronation of His Imperial Majesty Nicholas Pavlovich. Reaching Novgorod, I was granted leave on the mercy of the authorities and then in twenty days I came to the town of Klin in the Moscow province. Entering Moscow, I settled in our barracks and after several days, His Imperial Majesty the Emperor Nicholas I arrived, who was greeted by a parade comprised of all the Guard battalions and many army regiments. The Sovereign Emperor rode with Michael Pavlovich[32] and the rest of his suite on horseback while the Empresses Maria Feodorovna[33] and Alexandra Feodorovna[34] and the other princesses rode in eight variously and magnificently decorated carriages. The conclusion of the ceremony was announced with the ringing of bells, cheers from the people and cannon fire, and then the Sovereign rode to the Palace of Facets in the Kremlin.

---

31 Half the ribbon was Georgian (alternating two yellow or orange stripes with three black) and half was Andrean (pale sky blue), corresponding with the ribbons of the Orders of St. George and St. Andrew respectively. Александр Висковатов, *Историческое Описание Одежды и Вооружения Российских Войск*, vol. 18 (St. Petersburg: Военная Типография, 1860), pp.138-139 and plate 2580. [Alexandr Viskovatov, *Historical Description of the Dress and Armament of the Russian Army*, vol. 18 (St. Petersburg: Military Press, 1860), pp.138-139 and plate 2580.]

32 The fourth son of Emperor Paul I, and brother to Alexander I and Nicholas I.

33 Empress Consort to Paul I and mother of Emperors Alexander I and Nicholas I.

34 Empress Consort to Nicholas I.

Medal 'For the Capture of Paris, 19 March 1814'. Victory commemoration for participants. Plain silver. Half light-blue and half orange and black ribbon. Viskovatov, *Historical Description of the Dress and Armament of the Russian Army* (St. Petersburg: Military Press, 1860), Vol 18, Plate 2580.

On the 22nd of August [3rd of September], the Emperor was crowned and silver medallions the size of a *dvugrivennik* were distributed with the inscription 'Nicholas I', which I received.[35] On the 21st of September [3rd of October], we left Moscow for St. Petersburg and on the 24th [6th of October] we passed through the city of Klin again where, by the mercy of my superiors, I was released again to my family home on the Day of the Intercession of the Theotokos[36] and on that day I had the pleasure of seeing my family again, staying with them until the 5th [17th] of October. After leaving home, I caught up with the company in the town of Valday, returned to St. Petersburg, was received in the city by the Emperor and retired to our barracks.

On the 3rd [15th] of April, 1828, our whole Guard Corps was sent to the Danube where it marked the border with Turkey. On the 27th of June [9th of July], we crossed the river into the Turkish possessions and travelled by way of the fortress Isaccea, the town of Babadag, along the shore of the Black Sea, past the fortress of Constanta, the towns of Mangalia and Kavarna, and finally the fortress of Varna, from where, due to a fever, I was sent to the city of Sevastopol in Crimea on the 13th [25th] of September.[37] When departing from the fortress of Varna aboard a ship on the Black Sea, a powerful storm struck and continued all during my painful illness,

---

35 A *dvugrivennik* or *dvugrivennyy* was a silver coin worth 20 kopecks, one fifth of a ruble, with an approximate diameter of 22 mm. A *grivennik* was a ten-kopeck coin. Andreyevskiy et al., *Brockhaus and Efron Dictionary*, s.v. 'Гривенник'. [Ibid., s.v. 'Grivennik'.]

36 1 (13) October.

37 Nazarov's evacuation coincided with the arrival of the Ottoman army under Pasha Omer Vrioni, which the Russians drove off in an attack on the 16 [28] September, 1828. Gulevich, *Leib-Guard Finland Regiment*, Vol. 2, pp.60-73.

Medal 'For the Turkish War' of 1828-1829. Victory commemoration for participants. Plain silver. Orange and black ribbon. Viskovatov, *Historical Description of the Dress and Armament of the Russian Army* (St. Petersburg: Military Press, 1862), Vol.30, Plate 1351.

killing twelve men: ten by knocking them overboard and two were dashed on the shore. I was sure I was about to die but God delivered me from death and destruction. When I arrived in Sevastopol, I was sent to the Aleksandrovskiy Hospital, where I stayed until February. Upon my recovery, I returned to the regiment on the 18th [30th] of March, 1829 at their billeting in the village of Glovanevsk in the Kamenets-Podolskiy province. And from there, on the 24th [5th of April] we relocated to the village of Smelo, in the Kiev province.

We departed from there on the 28th of October [9th of November] and reached St. Petersburg on the 10th [22nd] of February, 1830. Travelling through Kiev, we spent two days there and a dinner was arranged for us by the community. During those two days I visited the holy sites, such as the Monastery of the Caves, and departed early in the morning. In the monastery we wanted to hold a thanksgiving prayer to the miraculous image of the Pecherskaya Mother of God and, having each bought a candle, we went into the Caves of Saint Anthony to see the holy relics with the guidance of a monk showing us their resting place. We had lagged behind him out of curiosity and another monk collecting a different party of worshipers came upon us. From him we learned that we were locked in the cave, since our party came out already and did not know they had left us behind. We thought we were still following behind them. Such a wonder surprised me, because the time we spent seemed so short yet our fellows already completed the circuit and entered another cave while we were still in the first, but to our good fortune another monk came past where we were stuck while escorting a merchant and generously took us to venerate the holy relics of the monks in the second cave. I also visited the monastery of the Great Martyr Barbara[38] and the church of Andrew the First-Called. *Devotion is surprising for a Pesant* *soldier*

We departed from Kiev for Cherigov, then to Smolensk, Staraya Russa, and Novgorod. We stayed in barracks in the village of Izhora and received medals depicting a radiant Holy Cross above a crescent moon as is used in mosques in place of our cross with the inscription 'For the Turkish War of 1828 and 1829'. We entered St. Petersburg as a parade and were greeted by the Emperor Nicholas and all the citizens.

IV

In 1831, we participated in the campaign against the Polish rebels. We crossed the border into the Tsardom of Poland on the 24th of February [12th March] as a part of the expedition to prevent the rebels from crossing the Rivers Bug and Narew and to pursue them. From the 22nd to the 26th of March [3rd to 7th of April], we moved from Ostroleka to Przetycz and from the 28th to the 30th of March [9th to 11th of April] we returned to Ostroleka again. From the 9th [21st] to the 12th [24th] of April, we moved to the village of Wasewo, then to Nur on the 13th [25th] and back to Ostroleka again from the 20th to the 23rd [2nd to 5th of May]. We returned to Przetycz on the 1st [13th] of May and then retreated through Tykoczyn to the Narew River. From the 4th to the 9th [16th to 21st] of May, some battles were fought: on the 6th [18th] at the village of Sokolow-Podolski and Stara Jakac, and on the 8th [20th] in the woods around Rudka, where I was wounded by a bullet passing straight through my right leg, damaging bones and veins, for which I was awarded the soldier's medal of the Order of Saint George, No. 64,665.[39]

When I received this wound, I fell to the ground and felt as though my leg had been blown off at the knee and could not walk for more than a few paces, but seeing a large tree nearby, I forced myself towards it and hid behind it for cover, laying there until evening. All around me the battle raged on relentlessly. Many from our company were killed and wounded. Cannon fire and shouts of 'ura' drowned out everything and created some kind of strange and incomprehensible churning of the world that was horrifying to see. Suddenly a soldier from our company went

---

38 The reliquary to St. Barbara was housed in the Golden-Domed Monastery of St. Michael. Andreyevskiy et al., *Brockhaus and Efron Dictionary*, s.v. 'Златоверхий Михайловский монастырь.' [Andreyevskiy et al., *Brockhaus and Efron Dictionary*, s.v. 'St. Michael's Golden-Domed Monastery.']

39 The 'mark of distinction', 'soldier's cross' or 'Georgian cross' was a medal created in 1807 within the Order of St. George to be awarded to private soldiers, sailors, and non-commissioned officers for bravery in combat, as before only officers were eligible to the four classes of the chivalric order. It was a silver cross resembling the officer's fourth class but with an embossed image and no coloured enamel. In 1856, Nicholas I expanded the soldiers' award into four grades of its own. Complete Collection of Laws, collection 1, Vol. 29, pp.1013-1016. No. 22,455.; Ibid., collection 2, Vol. 31, pp.132-134. No. 30,274.

Mark of Distinction of the Order of Saint George for privates and non-commissioned officers. Bravery in battle. Plain silver. Orange and black ribbon. *Viskovatov, Historical Description of the Dress and Armament of the Russian Army* (St. Petersburg: Military Press, 1860), Vol. 18, Plate 2579.

past me with a captured Pole in tow and when they saw me, he stopped and asked if I could walk but I replied that I could do nothing. He took my equipment off me and put them on over his greatcoat, took his prisoner to the clearing by the village of Rudka and saw two of my fellow soldiers. The four of them then carried me to the village and laid me on the road on top of my greatcoat and looked up to see the Poles ahead already firing at us. Because they had nowhere else to carry me, they said 'what can we do with you? If we leave you with the enemy behind us, you'll be bayonetted to death'. I began to cry and they cried over me, saying 'we have to put you in a house or they'll crush you on the road'. The night was becoming dark. I begged them through my tears not to leave me in danger and badly injured and though they cried with me, alas, they did not know what to do. It saddened them greatly that they could not take me anywhere safely and had to leave me, but I decided to let them go and made for the house myself.

Suddenly the brigade and detachment commander appeared,[40] and with him was a comrade of mine who requested permission to carry me, wounded as I was,

---

40   The 4th Guard Infantry Brigade, then containing the *Leib*-Guard Jäger and Finland Regiments, was commanded by Major General Stepan Grigoryevich Poleshko. Gulevich, *Leib-Guard Finland Regiment*, Vol. 2, p.137.

and took a bench to lay me on, which he did when he was granted permission. After some time, the 8th Jäger Company caught up with us.

The sergeant major asked: 'which company are you from and who is the wounded?' My comrades answered 'Pamfil Nazarov'. He heard this and ordered eight of his men to carry me, because he knew me and my comrades returned from whence they came. I was carried as if I were dead. After carrying me for some distance, they were ordered to halt and repel the enemy, placing me on a road, and my comrades did not know whether to take me somewhere else or leave me there. During such lamentable circumstances, a captain suddenly approached looking for the captain of our company and had brought a horse. He asked who the wounded man was and they answered with my name. He immediately put me on the horse and I parted with my comrades as if I were dying, so desperate was I to see them alive and they me. We rode to a *karczma* (which is what they call a tavern) two *versta*s [2.13 km] away where aid had been prepared for the wounded with carts, doctors and barbers but as we learned that the carts had been stolen by the wounded, the captain was forced to take me to another tavern. The next was empty and we went on to a third at a distance of three *versta*s [3.2 km] where we found many wounded and a doctor, a barber and carts prepared to send the wounded to Bialystok.

I was put on one of the wagons, but the barber and some assistants approached and ordered me be taken into the tavern for dressing my wound. I knew that my leg would be taken so I did not let them carry me. He complained to the doctor, who came over and asked me to allow them to take me, but I told the doctor that I would only let them bandage me there on the cart, since it would be hard to move from place to place. Hearing me, he ordered the barber to dress me on the wagon and we set off to the town of Tykoczyn, where from a lack of food and loss of blood I caught a strong fever and a thirst. Several times I drank foul and muddy water from the wheel ruts, since clean water was nowhere to be found. Passing this town, the bridge over the river was set alight and our forces began a battle with the enemy, in which several of our regiment died.[41]

Continuing on for no more than 5 *verst*s [5.33 km], we stopped our carts to feed the horses and cooked a meal for ourselves and when my comrades learned where I was, I came over and said goodbye as if I were dying. I cannot remember anything of it and only learned about it later. That was when my boots were carried off and I was left with just one shirt and a bloody greatcoat, as my backpack was left on the battlefield, which contained my state-issued items and such. For example: my medals for the Turkish War and the capture of Paris, my book of Psalms and my spare shirts. We continued on to Bialystok, where I was admitted into a hospital. I was given

---

41 The engagement at Tykoczyn was fought on 9 [21] May. Gulevich, *Leib-Guard Finland Regiment*, Vol. 2, pp.107-115.

nothing more to eat than oatmeal kissel[42] and a few spoonsful of honey. I was laid up for three weeks and then I was given a pair of crutches, which enabled me to go outside and get some fresh air. Once at 5 in the morning, I slipped on my crutches, fell and broke my leg even worse, forcing me to lie in bed for six more weeks.

Now my wounds had healed, but the swelling and aching was worse than ever. The doctor thought that some substance was remaining which failed to drain from the wound, so he ordered that an ointment from oil of vitriol be applied to a clean area above the knee and release the substance. As soon as it was put on, it began to burn like fire and I went crazy and became sick, but I eventually gathered my strength to go out again and sit on a rock. A soldier-labourer issuing food to patients saw me and asked 'have you had anything to eat?' But I replied that I had not because the poison was hard at work and I was nauseous and felt like my head was spinning. He told me to undo my dressing and wipe away the ointment. When I returned to my bed in the hospital, I followed his advice and opened my dressing to see that the flesh looked exactly like a burned coal. I took a knife and cut it out without feeling any pain and made a wound the size of a dove's egg. A sergeant major of a Jäger regiment, learning of this, gave me a cheap olive oil and made a dressing for the wound with which to apply it. From this, I recovered much better though in six weeks the mass still did not recede.

The chief doctor visited and I requested that he grant me some leeches but he was offended by this and had me put under arrest on bread and water, believing that I should learn from him how to treat my injury. As soon as he left the room, I said I would bring a complaint to His Highness[43] when he visited the hospital, but a barber-surgeon was in the room and he warned the doctor about what I had said. On hearing this, the doctor ordered that I be given full portion meals again. The doctor was ordered to assess our disabilities and upon inspection, filed papers to His Highness who then assigned me to the Guard Invalids. He ordered that I be discharged to our barracks, where I stayed until spring.

On the 28th of May [9th of June], 1832, an order was given by His Highness to present us in St. Petersburg, and we were given two carts for transit. Arriving in Tsarskoe Selo, I was greeted by another wounded man already in the invalids who hugged me like a friend and congratulated me on the grace of the sovereign, telling me that a Georgian cross had been sent from the regiment to the invalids for me and had been waiting there for more than half a year. I could not believe his words. We in the Guard Invalids arrived in St. Petersburg and were sent to the brigade

42   A kind of gelatinous porridge made by partially fermenting cereals and sometimes fruit juice. Andreyevskiy et al., *Brockhaus and Efron Dictionary*, s.v. 'Кисель, кушанье'. [Andreyevskiy et al., *Brockhaus and Efron Dictionary*, s.v. 'Kissel, a dish.']

43   Nazarov refers to the Grand Prince Michael Pavlovich, the Emperor's youngest brother, who was head of the Guard Corps from after Constantine Pavlovich died in 1831 until his own death in 1849. Constantine's death also meant that the Finland Regiment received a new chief, the then four-years-old Constantine Nikolayevich. Gulevich, *Leib-Guard Finland Regiment*, Vol. 2, pp.85-126.

chancellery, where a section non-commissioned officer came to me and embraced me when he learned of my arrival. He burst into tears of joy for the fact that God had granted we see each other again and congratulated me but I still could not believe anyone's words. He assured me and said: 'as surly as God is holy, you have been delivered to us and there is a cross for your chest'. I wiped away my tears and thanked God that I would be allowed such benevolence. From the brigade chancellery we were sent back to Tsarskoe Selo to the regimental commander, from whom I received my Georgian cross, and he personally assigned me to the Guard's 2nd Invalid Company,[44] to which I walked with a non-commissioned officer on crutches. → what was the Cross for???

After walking only a *versta* [1.07 km], I had to sit down on the road and could not go any further, but to our fortune a gardener rode by pulling a cart of manure and we began to ask him to carry us. He agreed, and we rode to the town of Pavlovsk, five *versta*s [5.33 km] down the road.

In November of 1832, in the 2nd Invalid Company at Pavlovsk, I was ordered to ride to St. Petersburg to retrieve a chest of items. While crossing the Chude Bridge on crutches, I slipped and fell, hurting my wounded knee, so that several times I had to lie up on the side of the road like a milestone. I felt sick and my heart sank. In the wounded knee I felt a break and swelling. Reaching with great difficulty the infirmary of the Finland Regiment, twelve leeches were put on my wounded knee and all night I had a barber-surgeon and my good friend Ivan Ivanovich by me. He was very sorry for my misfortune in receiving such a blow. That day, his comrades visited and among them was company commander Captain Naumov, who congratulated me on receiving the Order of Saint George the Bringer of Victory and awarded me a *chetvertak*,[45] saying to me: 'what did you think, that I forgot you? I could never forget your service, which is sacred to me'.

When I returned to Pavlovsk and my company, I was sent to the Police Board to watch over a guard detachment in place of a *Gefreiter*[46] and served in that company until the 23rd of December, 1834 [4th of January, 1845], the day on which I was granted retirement as indefinite leave.[47]

---

44 Ordinarily, invalids from the Finland Regiment were assigned to Guard Invalid Company No. 10. Gulevich, *Leib-Guard Finland Regiment*, Vol. 2, p.68; Viskovatov, *Historical Description of Dress and Armament*, vol. 19, pp.253-256.

45 A 25-kopeck coin, one quarter of a ruble. Also known as a 'Polupoltinnik' – 'half of a half-ruble'. Andreyevskiy et al., *Brockhaus and Efron Dictionary*, s.v. 'Полуполтинник.'; Andreyevskiy et al., *Brockhaus and Efron Dictionary*, s.v. 'Четвертак, русская монета.' [Andreyevskiy et al., *Brockhaus and Efron Dictionary*, s.v. 'Polupoltinnik.'; Ibid., s.v. 'Chetvertak, Russian coin.']

46 A senior private entrusted with the leadership of a small detachment or guard. The title was an informal post and not an established rank yet in the Russian Imperial Army during the Napoleonic era. Andreyevskiy et al., Brockhaus and Efron Dictionary, s.v. 'Ефрейтор.' [Andreyvskiy et al., Brockhaus and Efron Dictionary, s.v. 'Yefreytor.']

47 By law, conscription was for a term of 25 years. Nazarov's leave effectively cut his service by three years. *Complete Collection of Laws*, Collection 1, Vol. 23, p.459. No. 17149.

When arriving in St. Petersburg, I was pleased to watch His Highness, and in the morning the Emperor himself, at the Mikhaylovskiy Manège, where the Empress Alexandra Feodorovna and her daughter Maria Nikolayevna arrived. The Emperor chose to ride alongside their carriage on horseback. The Sovereign rode around a line formation and the soldiers ceaselessly cried *ura*! He stopped in the centre of the arena and watched platoons and columns pass. After the last, His Majesty ordered them to stop and approached to say farewell to us with tears in his eyes, thanking us for our loyalty and bravery. He asked that those of us departing would come forward and greet him. There were around 5,000 of us, and this discharge was named 'The Cavaliers', since all of us without exception were cavaliers[48] by the time of the opening of the monument to the eternal memory of Alexander I[49]. We said farewell to the Emperor, Empress, and their daughter and remained in the square while His Highness asked us to surround him. He thanked us for our bravery and longstanding service and then said a final farewell to us with teary eyes.

V

Receiving indefinite passes, we went wherever we pleased, but I chose to stay in St. Petersburg.[50] No longer holding a position, I rented an apartment for ten rubles a month and lived in it for six weeks. When I found a position at the Kazan Cathedral, I moved there. I learned about a friend that held a position there for more than two years and he recommended me to the protopriest so that I could gain a place there. After serving for several days at the cathedral, I went to the Highest Committee, where I was examined by several general members and doctors, and was awarded a pension until my death of 80 paper rubles per year. Sometime later, I received the medal of the Order of St. Anne for twenty years of unblemished service.[51] Then I went to the Church of Simeon and Anna where I gave thanks to God for the award

---

48 A recipient of a chivalric order – for enlisted men this typically meant either the cross of St. George for bravery or the medal of St. Anne for 20 years of 'unblemished' service. *Complete Collection of Laws*, Collection 1, Vol. 30, p.138. No. 22,903.

49 The Alexander Column was revealed on 30 August [11 September], 1834 in the Palace Square in St. Petersburg. Andreyevskiy et al., *Brockhaus and Efron Dictionary*, s.v. 'Александровская колонна.' [Andreyevskiy et al., *Brockhaus and Efron Dictionary*, s.v. 'Alexander column.']

50 When Nazarov was conscripted, a junior private in the Guard was nominally paid 13 rubles 46½ kopecks per year, and a senior private was paid 22 rubles 2 ½ kopecks a year. *Complete Collection of Laws*, Collection 1, Vol. 43, part 2, pp.134-135.

51 The medal of the Order of St Anne for enlisted men and NCOs consisted of a small gilded silver disc with a red cross in the center, surrounded by a red circle and supplanted by an etched crown. The ribbon suspending the medal was the same as for the chivalric degrees of the order: red with thin yellow bands along both edges. Viskovatov, *Historical Description of Dress and Armament*, Vol. 9, p.127 and plate 1273.

Mark of Distinction of the Order of Saint Anne for privates and non-commissioned officers. 20 years of unblemished service. Gilded silver with red enamelling. Red and yellow ribbon. Viskovatov, *Historical Description of the Dress and Armament of the Russian Army* (St. Petersburg: Military Press, 1851), Vol.9, Plate 1273.

from the Tsar. I also received the Polish cross for military honour, which had the Latin inscription 'Militari Virtuti' or 'for military virtue' on it.[52]

On my transferal from company to company and on my postings I will say that from conscription I was recorded as in the 8th Jäger Company but when I joined the regiment in Prussia during the truce, I was selected by the regimental commander for the 6th Jäger Company and in 1815 I was chosen by Colonel Akhlestyshev for the Sharpshooter Platoon of the 2nd Carabinier Company, where I served for no more than two years before being chosen as a section treasurer. The non-commissioned officer of the section, containing more than 50 people, called a vote and asked 'whom do you want to elect as the treasurer?' They all answered 'Pamfil Nazarov'. This was unwanted news when I heard of it and I asked to be released of the burden, as I knew that the post could be very risky. The NCO assembled the section again and asked them if they would release me but they answered 'we want him'. I teared up and retired to my bed but they followed me, grabbed me by the arms and shook me, shouting '*ura!*' I held this post for five years. I took part in company drill in the same company I was in previously, which was commanded

---

52 Nicholas I decreed on 31 December, 1831 [12 January, 1832] that the Polish Order of Military Virtue be used to award the participants in the campaign to supress the November Uprising. The medal of the order's 5th class was given to enlisted men and barber-surgeons: a silver cross with a wreath surrounding the Polish eagle and 'MILI – VIR – TUTI – TARI' printed on the four arms. The ribbon was dark blue with black stripes along its edges. Viskovatov, *Historical Description of Dress and Armament* Vol. 30, pp.291-292 and plate 1352; *Complete Collection of Laws*, Collection 2, Vol. 6, pp.357-358. No. 5049.

Polish Order of Military Virtue, 5th Class. Repurposed into a victory commemoration for privates and NCOs participating in supressing the November Uprising of 1830-1831. Plain silver. Dark blue and black ribbon. Reverse Latin reads "King and Country" and S-A-R-P stands for Stanislaus Augustus, King of Poland, who founded the original Polish Order of Military Virtue in 1792. Viskovatov, *Historical Description of the Dress and Armament of the Russian Army* (St. Petersburg: Military Press, 1862), Vol.30, Plate 1352.

by a lieutenant of a different company and he often repeated to me to keep my eyes right even when it meant staring into the sun. When I could stand the pain in my eyes no longer, he came over to me and struck me on the cheek so hard that I will never forget it. That same lieutenant taught us bayonet drill in our barracks and noticed that I did not lunge the same as my comrades, due to my injury. He thought I was holding back out of laziness and struck me on the back so hard that I fell onto a bench with my musket.

In March of 1826, His Imperial Majesty Nicholas I chose to inspect us in a riding hall and chose me to be assigned to the 2nd Jäger Company in the 1st Battalion. That week, we were ordered to depart St. Petersburg to the town of Oranienbaum, a distance of 35 *verstas* [37.34 km] to mount a guard, and were quartered in the homes of the town. While waiting for Easter Sunday, I cried beyond comfort, having been separated from my friends. And on that day when even the birds and animals would rejoice and be happy, I was sad.

Staying until autumn in that town, we were ordered back to St. Petersburg, I had to visit the 2nd Battalion of our regiment as the remaining provisions for our battalion were to be augmented by each of the companies of that battalion, and I was entrusted with the task. Gathering all of the supplies, it was ordered to keep watch over me until the battalion arrived and all the while I was there, I was dreadfully afraid – being alone in the barracks, far from town and surrounded by forest. When the provisions were secure, I set out to the town of Kronstadt, where I stayed for a day, and then travelled to St. Petersburg on a ferry. Paying 80 kopecks, I covered 25 *verstas* [26.67 km] in two hours. After returning to the company and spending a few days with them, the company elder and treasurer was sacked due to poor health and another election was held to find someone else worthy of it.

For that reason, Captain Rumyantsev gathered the company and asked 'whom do you want for the position of the elder?' They replied 'Pamfil Nazarov'. I accepted this and served in that post until I was dismissed into the Invalids.

On the 4th of January, 1836, I received a passport and stayed at the Kazan Cathedral until April, then hired a cart and left for my parents' home, arriving there at 4 in the afternoon on Lazarus Sunday.[53] I stayed with them until Easter but spent Saint Nicholas' Day with other relatives,[54] the Feast of the Ascension with my sister, and the Pentecost with my uncle.[55] Over several days I confided in them that I would not be staying with my family for very long because I intended on taking the tonsure and devoting myself to monasticism. They were grieved when they heard this from me. I stayed with them until the 1st [13th] of July and then left for Moscow and from there went on to Saint Sergius' Monastery. My mother and brother Mikhaylo, my two nieces Vasilisa Mikhaylovna and Matrena Ivanovna, and my dear goddaughter Nastasya Mikhaylovna accompanied me on the way. After hearing the Divine Liturgy, I went back with them over two *verstas* [2.13 km] and a few of them cried. We parted ways with great sorrow for all of us, but my goddaughter said goodbye with 'our beloved! How could we forget you?' Such words touched me deeply and I parted from them no more than a quarter of a *versta* [266.7 m], turned around, and bowed to them one last time, but in my sorrow I fell to the ground. As I reached the field of the monastery, I felt a strong sorrow and asked for the saint's intercession in easing my pain.

Coming to my quarters, I could not stay long, but dropping off my bag, I went to the monastery and when I saw a troika of horses, I asked the driver 'where are you going?'

He said: 'straight down the postal road to Pereslavl', which was a distance of 35 *verstas* [37.34 km]. Riding with him and spending the night, I got up in the morning and continued on foot to arrive in Pereslavl during late Mass at the Fedorovskiy Nunnery, where a consecration took place with Archimandrite Photius, having

---

53   Lazarus Saturday is the day before Palm Sunday, one week before Easter. Since Easter fell on 29 March [10 April] in 1836 for the Orthodox Church, then Palm Sunday was 22 March [3 April]. 'Православный календарь,' *Вечернюю Песнь*, accessed July 30, 2016. ['Orthodox Calendar,' *Evening Canto*, http://www.canto.ru/calendar/day.php?date=10-4-1836, accessed July 30, 2016.]

54   9 [21] May. Not to be confused with the winter festival on 6 [18] December.

55   Being 50 days after Easter, the Orthodox Pentecost fell on 22 June [4 July] in 1836.

come from Novgorod with the Countess [Anna Alekseyevna] Orlova. I received a blessing from him, continued on my way for 12 *verstas* [12.8 km] and then slept.

After awaking and continuing for several *verstas*, a wolf crossed my path which I did not notice until I was within two *sazhens* [4.27 m] of it, but God delivered me from danger and I reached the town of Petrov. I bought a pair of bast shoes there and when I put them on, I was shocked by the sight, as I had not worn shoes of bast in almost 25 years.[56] Reaching the Yakovlevskiy Monastery in Rostov at 8 in the evening, I spent the night in a hotel and was very tired, going to bed without eating or drinking anything. In the morning I prayed to Saints Jacob and Demitrius, visited the cathedral for early Mass, and then took part in a prayer to Lentius and Ignatius. I bought a ring of bread to eat and saw a troika pulling passengers to Yaroslavl, with whom I rode to that provincial capital on the 9th [21st] of June and spent the night at a coaching inn on the Kotorosl River.

The next morning, I went to the Spasskiy Monastery[57] and met Father Adrian who conducted Matins and let me stay in his cell until the 13th [25th]. I asked him about everything and learned that the post is not one of idleness and the penitence of a novice was very severe, but I, as a cripple, could not endure such penitence, which is why I immediately sought a cart back to Moscow. Finding one and giving a down payment of 80 kopecks, I went to say goodbye to Father Adrian during the time of evening Mass and went with him back to his cell to retrieve my things but before we could, we were both summoned by the Archbishop Abraham.

Seeing me, his High Eminence said 'you look familiar'. I told him that on several occasions I was worthy enough to receive blessings from him when he was in St. Petersburg. He turned back to Father Adrian and asked 'have you told me about this?' Father Adrian answered, and then the Archbishop asked me 'where do you wish to go?' I answered that I was incapable of the hardships required of the office, and since there were no easier vacancies, I wished to return to Moscow. But he said to me with a humble voice: 'serve my Pecherskaya Mother of God'.[58] On hearing these words I began to tear up and dropped to his feet, hearing someone ask me whom I would serve. I considered myself unworthy of even a shred of the archpastor's generosity but staying in the city was very expensive for me so I decided [to accept]. Suddenly the Archbishop called for a scribe and gave the order, taking my passport and writing in it the request for and subsequent acceptance into the monastic life, and in that same hour I was sent to the consistory. That was on

---

56 Bast is a material made from strips of the soft inner bark of trees which are then woven like wicker to make shoes, baskets, decorative art, etc. Andreyevskiy et al., *Brockhaus and Efron Dictionary*, s.v. 'Лыко.' [Andreyevskiy et al., *Brockhaus and Efron Dictionary*, s.v. 'Bast.']

57 Yaroslavl's Spaso-Preobrazhenskiy Monastery.

58 An icon produced at the Spaso-Preobrazhenskiy Monastery in 1823. Е. А. Поповицкий, ed., *Полный Православный Богословский Энциклопедический Словарь,*. (St. Petersburg: П. П. Сойкин, 1912), s.v. 'Печерская Ярославкая.' [E. A. Popovitskiy, ed., *The Complete Orthodox Theological Encyclopedic Dictionary.* (St. Petersburg: P. P. Soykin, 1912), s.v. 'Pecherskaya Yaroslavskaya.']

a Saturday, and on Sunday morning I held the position of candlebearer at the Preobrazhenskiy. During the second early Mass, I stood by the box and carried the paten, took collections in the church and approached the altar to fill the censer, an act which I was surprised would be necessary during early Mass. Everyone looked at me and wondered why a soldier-cavalier was more worthy of the candle than one of the elders. Such various duties continued unto the 28th of September [10th October]. That day, after early Mass, the Archimandrite came and commanded me to take a post of candlebearer at the Tolga Monastery and I was to be replaced where I was.

In June of 1839, the Archimandrite ordered me to make a petition to His Eminence Eugenius, which was submitted and sent to the Holy Synod in St. Petersburg and was accepted, allowing me to take the tonsure. But when the confirmation was received from St. Petersburg on the 23rd of September [5th November], His High Eminence thought it necessary to postpone my tonsure until Philip's Fast[59] on the grounds like the State of the Holy Fathers prescribed that one must fast for 40 days before being inducted into the monastic ranks, and due to my weakness, it was delayed until the 23rd of November [5 December].

VI

On the 22nd of November, 1839, passing all the brethren and begging for forgiveness and blessings, I went to the Archimandrite who sent me to the Bishop. When I came to him, I dropped to his feet and begged his forgiveness and blessing for the adoption of the angelic rank[60] and asked him to pour fervent prayers onto the Lord to strengthen me in my exploits, which I believed was necessary to save my soul. His Eminence, taking an icon of Saint Gennadius and blessing me with it, said: 'for some time I have wanted to see you in the angelic rank', and gave a book of Saint Varsonofius, adding: 'I give this to you to guide you for half a year, but then you will return it to me, for I need it as well'. Returning to my cell, I cried with joy and prepared for the ceremony. The next morning during early Mass, before the small entrance, I was tonsured by the Archimandrite Nicodemus in a large and warm chapel, while the Bishop stood by the window of the right

---

59   Also known as the Nativity Fast or the Advent, it begins 15 [27] November and ends 24 December [5 January].

60   A euphemism for monks of either the lesser or greater schema. The schema itself, Greek for 'form' or 'shape', as a mystery is the full and supreme monastic vow of asceticism and contemplation, but also refers to their garments. Monks of the full schema are distinguished by wearing the *analavos*, a narrow mantle densely decorated with images and acronyms describing the Passion of Christ. Andreyevskiy et al., *Brockhaus and Efron Dictionary*, s.v. 'Схима.'; Ibid., s.v. 'Параман.' [Andreyevskiy et al., *Brockhaus and Efron Dictionary*, s.v. 'Schema.'; Ibid.; s.v. 'Paramand.']

choir and oversaw my induction. Around me were four hieromonks,[61] Theoctistus, Theodoretus, Seraphim, and Macarius, who covered me with my mantle from the side of the parish. Reading the Canons of the Holy Fathers, a cypress cross was placed on me with the paramand, then the cassock and leather belt, then the cowl and mantle, sandals and *klobuk*.[62] In my left hand they gave a prayer rope, before me was placed an icon of the Saviour, and in my right hand a cross. Then in my left hand I took a candle with which I stood motionless through the whole Liturgy. After the Liturgy, the father took my candle and led me to receive Communion. I bowed to the altar and approached the Archimandrite to ask for his blessing, took the bread from him and was kissed with the greeting: 'Christ is among us, brother', which was repeated with all the bothers. I came to the Bishop who blessed me and gave me the counsel: 'pray to the Lord and be saved, and repeat often this prayer: "God be merciful to me, a sinner!"'

The Archimandrite led me back to the church in which there were a number of spectators and the Father was ordered to take me to his cell, giving me a candle and a cross, blessing the latter. I fell to his feet and asked him to not to abandon me in his prayers. In honour of my induction, a meal in solace was prepared for the brothers. The father read the lives of the saints and was ordered by the Bishop to release me from penitence for seven days, but to attend every service in the mantle. After the meal, they thanked me and returned to their cells. After this period, I resumed my duties.

My dear mother! I did not want to reveal to you the deeds which I suffered during my life, but by following the lead of my only singular love for you and my family and respect for your wisdom in age, and even the encouragement of yours and of my friends, do I disclose my life and open it to you.

I am your son and brother, your pilgrim-monk Metrophanes,
28th November [10th December], 1839.

VII

I will write again: as a boy, I once fell out of negligence from a shelf to the floor and hurt my head so badly that I passed out for several hours and the mark of this injury on my head is still quite palpable. The second time, I fell forward with a short bolt of cloth and badly bruised my chest. The third time, while standing on

---

61 Both a monk and priest; either a monk that had been ordained or a priest that had taken the tonsure. Andreyevskiy et al., *Brockhaus and Efron Dictionary*, s.v. 'Иеромонах. [Andreyevskiy et al., *Brockhaus and Efron Dictionary*, s.v. 'Hieromonk.']

62 A tall, cylindrical hat, the *kamilavkion*, with its veil, the *epanokalimavkion*, sewn onto it. Andreyevskiy et al., *Brockhaus and Efron Dictionary*, s.v. 'Клобук.' [Andreyevskiy et al., *Brockhaus and Efron Dictionary*, s.v. 'Klobuk.']

the platform above the oven, looking through the beams, it collapsed and I again hit my head on the floor.

I cannot keep silent about how much I am grateful to my mother. In the years of my youth, I was punished severely for my stubbornness. Although these punishments seemed severe at the time, I remain grateful for the correction of my disobedience, and at no time was I ever scolded worse than I deserved. Parents greatly need to correct their children in the youngest years into submission. Modest punishment gives youths both fear and love for their parents. This I learned from my own experience, and so I never fail to thank my parents for it. May you and all my family be saved by our Lord Jesus Christ. Pray for me, a sinner, and know that you will always be in my memory.

Forgive me,
Metrophanes.
1839.

The Recollections of Ivan Menshoy

I

For so long as we live, we learn, and we do not live as we wish, but as God commands it. Receiving a blessing, I wished to write my biography. Beginning where I can remember, I was about nine years old; we lived in the village of Streletskiy, in the county of Odoyev.[1] My parents were Minay Ivanovich and Feodisiya Larionovna Ostroukhov, peasants assigned to the Apukhtino-Archangelskiy parish, five *versta*s [5.33 km] from the county capital. They had eight children: four sons and four daughters, each smaller than the next, and all lived with their parents, being poor people. Later two of the daughters were married: Praskovya to Stepan Lukyanovich Bukanov in the same village, and Akulina to the merchant Semyon Tarasov in Odoyev. Our other two sisters Yevdokiya and Pelageya became novice nuns in the town of Belyov. The older brothers Ivan and Luka, being of age, were lent to a proprietor in Odoyev for several years and the two younger brothers Ivan (myself) and Mikhail lived at home.

I remember how I went to visit a tutor, the wife of the deacon at the Church of the Transfiguration, with whom I learned how to read Church Slavonic. I began to practice writing lines and then letters but I was a real rascal and lazy in my studies. Learning came easy to me and I began to write phrases, but I was sent back to the butcher Pankrutov in Odoyev to watch over the cattle he purchased for slaughter. Then I was given to protect a garden by the church in the village of Apukhtin, belonging to a merchant from Odoyev. Also sitting watch with me was a townsman from Odoyev who was once some big boss but had now fallen on hard times. I took the day shifts and he stood watch at night.

I was employed at that garden until autumn, when the merchant Maleyev (known to the commoners by the nickname Seledkin[2]) asked if I would like to live with him. I replied that I had parents and I would talk it over with them, and the merchant left. When the owner of the garden harvested the last of the apples, I went home with him. My mother met with Seledkin after several days and I was

---

1   Odoyev was in the Tula Governorate.
2   A surname meaning 'Herring-monger'.

given into his employ for a short while – for five years – and was indentured to serve him. Clothes and shoes were provided, but the whole five years was paid in advance and was only worth 25 rubles, coins or paper, in total: what a time that was! And now, in 1873, when I write these lines, a young man of the same age was crying over 12 silver rubles for a summer. I should note though at around 1806, everything sold cheaply: a *pud* [16.38 kg] of rye flour sold for 30 to 35 assignation rubles, a cow was worth two and a half rubles, and so on, and all for banknotes, as hard metal currency was rare.

Having lived in the town with the owner for a week, I went with him to the place of my future home. He kept a coaching inn twelve *verstas* [12.8 km] from Odoyev, in the village of Denisovo, which was near the town of Safanov.[3] We rode seven *verstas* [7.47 km] from the town and paused. Not far from the road stood a tall hazel tree and that year it grew large nuts. The owner sent me to pick them and I ran across and started to pluck them off the tree while singing 'ah my youth, o youth, how you've swiftly left me', and so on. My voice was very good then and the owner was also a young man who loved to sing. Once the picking was done, I ran and hopped onto the cart and we rode again, first chewing nuts as we went, but then I remember we sang a variety of songs and the owner led us with solos.

At last we arrived at the inn and the owner went inside while I unharnessed the horse and took him to the manger. I went into the inn, prayed to God and bowed to the staff: there were two employees named Yegor and Faddey.

'There you are', said the owner, 'the boy for recording debts and payments'. But how did I become a scribbler? Occasionally I would write in a book such that neither I nor the owner could make anything out and in the meantime I would read in order to memorize the sums and names recorded. I learned how to bake rolls, make soup, prepare slop for the pigs – this was all nothing compared to when I began to carry a tub of water which was beyond my capabilities as a child and caused me every difficulty. I did not grow very much, but I was stout. Regarding food all I will say is that it was in great abundance.

In the village was a manor house where there lived the venerable old steward Grigoriy Danilovich. It was required that I take a letter to him, but it could not be delivered by only my hand, so the gardener came to accompany me. He asked me to write and though I tried to explain I was unable, he insisted. Paper and ink were put on the table and I sat down. I wrote randomly and at a slant and made the old man burst out laughing. When the whole white page was covered in black ink, I left.

The next summer, a gentleman in a frock coat came to the inn and spent the night, and retired to bed without supper. We laughed and said 'he must be bitter

---

3   The Denisovo 12.8 km from Odoyev is closest to the town of Suvorovo. *Карманный Почтовый Атлас Российской Империи* (St. Petersburg: Депо Карт Его Императорского Величества, 1808), p.15. [*Pocket Postal Atlas of the Russian Empire* (St. Petersburg: His Imperial Majesty's Map Depot, 1808), p.15.]

about something and doesn't want to pay'. That day made me tired and I quickly fell asleep when I went to bed too. When we awoke in the morning, the gentlemen in the frock was gone and when we checked the treasury, the chest containing the money was missing. We ran across the yard looking for it and found it broken open and empty. Setting off in pursuit, the thief was caught and brought back. They began to search him and his pockets were so full of copper that if he did not keep hold of his trousers, they would fall to the floor from the weight. For all our grief, we began to laugh and when we confiscated the money, he cried at his guard that he was robbed. In our naivety, we were almost ready to return it to him out of fear, but thankfully the elder Yakov Muravyev, a resolute man, came to us. He angrily shouted: 'tie him up, the thief, and send him to the county court!' at which the gentleman began asking to be released. We gladly obliged his request and he was not as happy about it as we were.

Now I will describe the misdeed which my hosts did to me, though they cannot even remember it. My father had died and my mother asked them to release me so I could attend the funeral. I do not know what explanation they gave her, I only remember that they would not release me to travel a distance greater than 25 *verstas* [26.67 km]. Naturally I was a child then and did not feel a great sorrow that I could not attend my father's funeral, but now as I write these lines, despite the distance in time, it makes me very bitter.

By the mercy of God, I was pulled away from my five-year bondage, in the literal sense of the word, and was even sent home, but I did not live at home for very long. Mother sent me to the town of Belyov to the merchant Nikolay Ivanov[ich] Ulyanov for a year – I do not know how long I stayed with him, but it was less than a year. The old hostess was very angry and frequently hit me, so I complained to my mother. She took me away and sent me to a shop in the same town belonging to the merchant Mikhail Petrovich Skopin. That was in the autumn of 1812.

At this time, many French prisoners of war were driven through the town. They were barefoot and dressed in shambles: one was wrapped in a canvas, another wore a sack. It is difficult to imagine such a heart-breaking sight. Breads and rolls were thrown to them, even cabbage cores, and they fell over each other as they marched. They were eventually housed in taverns around the town. In one night many of them perished and they were buried in the cemetery together in the same grave. It happened that some French officers were placed with us; I brought them wooden cups and spoons and they bought and paid for them with coin. Despite my youth, my conversation with the prisoners made a large impression on me. I thought I might hurry myself into the army.

I lived out the year with the venerable Skopin. My older brothers Ivan and Luka joined the army as sutlers and I joined them. They began to assemble and purchase provisions and various remaining goods when a levy of recruits was announced. This frustrated our mercantile effort. My brothers began to distance themselves from me, apparently in the hope of dropping the burden on me, but they still did not have passports yet. The eldest brother Ivan was married and had two children and began to request that I release him by enlisting in the army and during this commotion the middle brother Luka slipped away with a forged pass. Only Ivan remained with us and I was afraid he would also abandon me. I do not know, but by some instinct (I will not say it was deliberate on my part because it was not), I kept an eye on my brother. Soon a letter from our mother was delivered to us by a courier, in which she wrote that she was arrested and shackled and would not be freed until one of her children fulfilled the levy. My heart began to boil: I thought at the time that if it were possible for me, I would pry off those irons from my mother's leg and leave my brother Ivan as payment. He had a large growth spurt of 13 *vershok*s [57.79 cm], but it did not make him any more of a man, thinking only of himself. I forgot to mention that my mother had hired three substitutes for the recruitment levy, but two were rejected for some reason and the third was accepted but changed his mind, and so they came for us.[4]

It was the second week of the Great Lent in 1813.[5] I asked my brother to take us to Odoyev but he said 'tomorrow', strung me along and fed me breakfasts. Seeing that these breakfasts would never end, I reminded him: 'why do we let our mother languish in irons? Today, certainly, we'll return home'. We hired horses, gathered our things, mounted up and drove off. In me there was not the slightest fear, yet my brother was a great coward.

While our brother Luka was with us, Ivan could still hope that maybe Luka would enlist, but the middle brother ran off, I was young and small in stature and Ivan could not muster his courage. And so we returned home. It was quite cold. Ivan drank some vodka and drove to a tavern at the request of a brother, though I knew nothing about it. He drank a large glass of vodka and offered me what seemed like a medical balm; as they say: 'vodka is the aunt of wine'. I did not feel well on the road.

We reached our home around midnight, banging with the knocker. When it unlocked for us, we rushed in to hug and kiss our mother. When we looked over the house, we saw our neighbour sitting on a horse, attired for keeping watch over our mother. I then took an axe and scythe, broke the restraints and threw them into the street, and the guardsman was sent to the chief to report our arrival. A drummer was lodged with us and I asked him to strike a signal for our arrival as well. When the drummer had struck up his beat and the watchman returned with

---

4   Conscription was by household, so the decision of which son to send was for the family to work out among themselves, but wealthier households could hire volunteers to take their place, so long as the position was filled and the recruits were physically acceptable. Andreyevskiy et al., *Brockhaus and Efron Dictionary*, s.v. 'Рекрутская повинность.' [Andreyevskiy et al., *Brockhaus and Efron Dictionary*, s.v. 'Obligation of recruitment.']

5   Great Lent in 1813 began on 17 [29] February, and the second week began on 23 February [7 March]. Easter was 13 [25] April. *Санктпетербургский Карманный Месяцеслов на лето от Рождества Христова 1813* (St. Petersburg: Императорская Академия Наук, 1813), p.3-8. [*St. Petersburg Pocket Menologium for the Year of Our Lord 1813* (St. Petersburg: Imperial Academy of Sciences, 1813), p.3-8.]

the head and elder of the parish, I remember then that a large group of people ran up to us, some with business and some just to watch. We wanted to take my brother Ivan in chains but he left the house, so they bound me instead and took me to another building.

I do not remember how long I sat. At some point it was revealed that our parish was commanded to definitely produce a recruit by the 1st [13th] of April. They began to assemble in Tula. I remember how my family wept, and my sister Pelageya cried the most. Tears flowed for three days before my departure for Tula. At first I kept my composure and had no doubt, but they reduced me to tears, so that I felt compelled to volunteer myself just to hurry my escape from that bitter scene. Finally the horses were fed and I was given a final kiss and a parting embrace.

How terrible was that minute! My mother and sisters lamented 'you'll be gone for twenty-five years' but the escort shouted to sit so I and all my family sat ourselves in the custom of our ancestors.[6] We rose again, prayed to God, and said our good-byes. I climbed onto a wagon and rode away.

Now, as I write these lines, after sixty years, already retired with the rank of captain and a cavalier, I cannot help but shed tears. We arrived in Krapivna for the night. Although I did not like alcohol, the proverb says 'a soldier drinks whether in joy or in grief', and I, being embroidered with grief, took another glass to drown my sorrows. We dined and retired to bed, and only in sleep could I forget and regain my strength. We were awoken by our handlers hungover, had a small meal for the road and then continued to Tula. At the coaching inn, my mother and brother Ivan visited me and we got drunk on *sbiten*[7] and vodka. Mother began to say to me 'Inyushka (as she called me), join the army for your brother; you are a bachelor and he is married with two children!' During these words, my brother rushed to my feet and she continued: 'The Lord will deliver you to happiness' while my brother remained lying at my feet waiting for my answer.

'I won't oppose you', I told her. 'If it's your wish, I'll go'. My brother was over-joyed and leapt up to kiss me and bought two bottles of wine. We squandered them and then retired to bed around midnight. The next day, we good youths were taken to be inspected, were stripped and put on the scales. The non-commissioned officer pulled me over and shouted 'three and a half *vershok*s [15.56 cm]!'[8] The gentleman said 'that won't do' and I in turn said that I would serve God and the

---

6   A Russian tradition called 'sitting on the path' entails all the members of a household sitting together in silence with their baggage for a moment before someone or everyone embarks on a long journey.

7   A boiled down drink made from honey, water or juice, spices, and sometimes alcohol, usually served hot. Andreyevskiy et al., *Brockhaus and Efron Dictionary*, s.v. 'Сбитень.' [Andreyevskiy et al., *Brockhaus and Efron Dictionary*, s.v. 'Sbiten.']

8   The 82nd Levy, decreed on 23 March [4 April], 1812 and applicable to all provinces, used height require-ments defined on 16 [28] September, 1811, which was 2 *arshin*s and 4 *vershok*s [160.02 cm]. Subsequent levies that year did not explicitly define new tolerances. If Ostroukhov stood 3.5 *vershok*s shy of the minimum height, then he would be 144.46 cm tall, or 4'9". *Complete Collection of Laws*, Collection 1,

great Sovereign willingly for my brother's sake. The doctor began to inspect me again and distrusted me like a gypsy, believing I was not healthy or that not all of my teeth were intact, even going so far as to reach into my mouth. He spoke with someone else briefly and then said 'he'll grow', turned around and shouted 'forehead, forehead, forehead!'

Here is a copy of a genuine receipt issued by the Tula Recruitment Board:

Receipt

On the 2nd of November, 1815, in accordance with the decree of HIH, the Tula Recruitment Board, Odoyev region, Arkhangelsko-Apukhtin parish, surroundings of the village of Streletskiy, observes that a recruit was delivered to the handler Maksim Stepanov prior to the 3rd of April, 1813 for fulfilling the assemblage as per eight men out of 500 souls, the 84th levy, and was found upon inspection to be fit for service for the assigned term. Money and provisions were appropriated to maintain the recruit's position in the general establishment. Into a detachment was sent the aforementioned recruit from Streletskiy, named Ivan Menshoy Minayev and eighteen years old; this recruit was presented with the aforementioned souls of the Odoyev region, Streletskiy village, these being 52 out of a number of 114, to which were joined a postscript of 7 recruits from around Kuznetsk, and 3 out of 35 from the village of Podromanovo, for a total of 62 souls.
  – Counselor Popov
  – Clerk Lebedev

The barber asked the handler for money, promising to do a better job, and was obliged, being ordered then to shear my forehead and shave my beard. We recruits were driven into the next room to swear an oath of allegiance to the service of the Tsar. After our oath, we were taken before the battalion commander. I recall him standing on a balcony high above and being visible to everyone in attendance. We were lined up in a single rank and a clerk began to call roll. When he reached my turn, he shouted 'Ivan Menshoy!' I did not answer. He repeated the name and still I kept silent. Finally he approached me and asked 'are you Ivan?' I said 'I'm Ivan, but not Menshoy. I'm Ostroukhov'. This all happened because we had two brothers named Ivan, one 'bolshoy' and one 'menshoy,'[9] and being the lesser of the two, it was necessary to be called Ivan Menshoy, a name that would seem to follow me to my grave. At this time, an officer in large epaulettes shouted from the balcony that Menshoy would be rejected, as were others, but when each rejected recruit was

---

Vol. 31, pp.840-842. No. 24,772 and 24,773.; Ibid., collection 1, vol. 32, pp.241-242. No. 25,052; Ibid., p.405. No. 25,198.; Ibid., pp.466-468. No. 25,279 and 25,280.

9   'Большой, bolshoy' – larger, older, senior; 'меньшой, menshoy' – smaller, younger, junior.

taken up to the balcony by the handlers and returned again into line, we were all accepted. All the while, my brother Ivan was standing at the gates and when the officer from the balcony shouted out that I was unfit, my brother became frightened, picked up his coat and disappeared.

We were taken to our quarters. My mother and brother came to visit me, and we drank together, I with grief but my brother with joy. To comfort me, my mother spent the night with us, but when I woke up the next day and saw myself in the mirror with my forehead shaved back, I was greatly shocked. I lay down, still looking at my reflection, meditated on it, and made the sign of the cross, saying 'Lord! Let your will be done!' A *Gefreiter* came to me and led me to rollcall. We were counted off and then returned to quarters. On the third or fourth day my mother and brother returned home. I walked them out, they left me some money, and we said our goodbyes. That was during Holy Week of 1813.[10]

A retired officer named Rudnev was assigned to us for leading our party on a march, during the week of St. Thomas.[11] We were joined by three men from Odoyev and we begged our officer that we be able to return home for Holy Week, and he graciously agreed to grant us leave, however I cannot remember if he allowed us to leave without passes or if he was more restrictive than that. We arrived in time for Holy Saturday,[12] attended Matins and the Liturgy, and broke our fast. My mother and all of the family were very happy with my return, and I had grown comfortable with our situation, staying for two weeks, before being compelled by orders to move to the city of Zhizdra. I parted again from my family and thought that it might be forever. They used to say that that the gates to the soldiery were wide, but the gates to return were narrow, yet it seemed quite the opposite.

II

We arrived in Zhizdra ahead of schedule, and the next day I approached our party's officer Rudnev to offer him a loaf of sugar and a *funt* [409.52 g] of tea. He took it very graciously and thanked me for arriving on time. I forget to say that from Odoyev to Belyov I left to visit my sister, Evdokiya Minayevna, who gave me three large golden imperials[13] and mended my coat under one of the arms. The next day I bid her farewell with many tears. I saved and stretched out my gold for a long, long time. Then we left Zhizdra to march to Bobruysk. In that city I bought

10   Palm Sunday in 1813 fell on 6 [18] April for the Russian Orthodox, and Holy Week begins the Monday after. *Pocket Menologium of 1813*, pp.3-8.
11   Also known as Antipascha, or the week after Easter which begins with Thomas (Foma) Sunday. In 1813 this fell on 20 April [2 May]. *Pocket Menologium of 1813*, pp.3-8.
12   The day before Easter Sunday, which in 1813 was 12 [24] April. *Pocket Menologium of 1813*, pp.3-8.
13   A ten-ruble coin minted in gold. Andreyevskiy et al., *Brockhaus and Efron Dictionary*, s.v. 'Империал.' [Andreyevskiy et al., *Brockhaus and Efron Dictionary*, s.v. 'Imperial'.]

two *funt*s [819 g] of Turkish tobacco and a pipe and on that day I took up smoking. There were no special adventures for me during the march except that in the forest we chased after squirrels and I lost my wallet with some of my money inside.

We arrived in Slonim. In this city, our party was divided into two: one half was chosen to join the army and the other half, which included me, proceeded to the town of Novogrudok. We were then told that we would join the Guard. The day after our arrival at Novogrudok, we were assembled in formation on the town square and were approached by a Colonel Pavlov from the *Leib*-Guard Uhlan Regiment. He was responsible for purchasing remounts and assigned us to the reserves of the various Guard regiments. He assigned me to the *Leib*-Guard Dragoon Regiment. When he finished assigning us, he suddenly remembered about asking for singers and I was counted among them too. We singers were then all assigned to the *Leib*-Guard Uhlan Regiment and sent to the reserve squadrons.

Our uhlan squadron was billeted in the county of Bielsk [Podlaski] in the Bialystok *oblast*. The commander of the squadron was Captain[14] Roman Grigorevich Glazenap. We were divided into two platoons and I was assigned to the second. Each platoon received thirty or more horses but there were no more than six men each. The new horses were all Dons and wild. Trained horses were three each and experienced soldiers were two each, and the latter were detrimental for the recruits since they would only go off to the tavern and get drunk. Time and time again I cried in frustration: so many horses that we needed to clean, lead to water, feed and so on, and the horses would never let us get close to them, striking at us every minute. Their wildness could be judged by their harnesses on two belts of raw hide and rings like a bear's, their reins were just a little thinner than an anchor line and all the horses had broken their tethering posts. We recruits had to tend to these kinds of beasts.

Little by little we became accustomed to the horses and they to us. Our reserve was joined by veterans returning from hospital and new recruits, reaching forty men in the platoon, and everyone was reorganized almost every day, such that another squadron was split off from ours and was assigned to march to Paris. That new squadron was appointed a Staff-Captain[15] Vyndomskiy as its commander and I was also asked to ride with them, but I felt miserable having to leave Glazenap.

---

14 Captains in the cavalry used a term borrowed from either the archaic German *Rotmeister* (now *Rittmeister*) or Polish *rotmistrz* but were equal to captains in the infantry and artillery. Shepelyov, *Titles, Uniforms and Orders*, pp.117-118.]

15 'Staff-Rittmeister' A rank below a full captain and above lieutenant. In the regular complement of a field regiment, the rank appeared in squadrons nominally led by senior officers (major to colonel) or the regimental chief (usually a general), to lead when that officer was absent from his squadron. Shepelyov, *Titles, Uniforms and Orders*, pp.117-118.; *Complete Collection of Laws*, Collection 1, Vol. 43, Part 2 (1801-1810), p.124.; *Его Императорского Величества Воинский Устав о Полевой Кавалерийской Службе* (St. Petersburg: Государственная Военная Коллегия, 1797), pp.1-6. [*His Imperial Majesty's Military Regulations on the Field Cavalry Service* (St. Petersburg: State Military Collegium, 1797), pp.1-6.]

Vyndomskiy's squadron set off for Paris and I cared for the horses and equipment, quickly becoming proficient at it like an old soldier. All the reserves were put under the command of General of Cavalry Kologrivov, who was quartered in Bielsk. Our squadron was again reinforced with new men and, in the beginning of 1814, it reached its full complement but without officers. We were assigned to the town of Bielsk to mount a guard; and how fun that was! Despite being only a recruit myself, I was assigned to the *Hauptwacht*[16] in the place of an officer.

We were heavily and repetitively drilled, but how well we executed our manoeuvres I cannot say; I believe we only barely succeeded in what was expected of us. Again we assembled and travelled to the town of Bielsk, where the next day there was a rehearsal parade, but we marched past in such a poor state that I cannot recall the memory without laughing. On the third day, there was a posting ceremony during which there was played music I cannot name and never heard again since, but was from some cuirassier regiment. After the ceremony, I was put on guard duty again, replacing a cuirassier officer. I will say that I was clever and not shy, but in that matter I was still, as they say, an ignoramus. Six cuirassiers were detained at the guardhouse; of what they were guilty, I did not know. Seeing me as just a stupid boy, they began asking me to let them visit the nearby inn, on account of the fact it was Holy Week.[17] Being ignorant of military law, I bent to their heavy request and paroled them on their words of honour. Even now, I shudder from the stupidity. I went out to look for them, like the fool that I was, but thanks to God and the honour of those prisoners, they all returned to the guardhouse on their own – drunk, of course. I was greatly happy and relieved. Thank God, my guard ended safely and we changed places again with the cuirassiers but without any ceremony, then we retired to our quarters.

A damned fever took me, and our farrier treated me with some foul remedy that was torturous and offered no relief. I was assigned to teach other recruits in marching and the movements of the sabre, but due to my illness, the training was poor. Every day of the training was marred by my fever. At the end of May, we were sent to march to St. Petersburg. With my illness, sitting in the saddle was still only just tolerable and riding terrified me. The squadron moved to Vilno and I accompanied the baggage train. We stayed in that city for six days and my fever passed, allowing me to ride again.

16 'Main watch' – the primary guard posting which is responsible for other smaller posts and pickets around a town, fortress, or camp. Andreyevskiy et al., *Brockhaus and Efron Dictionary*, s.v. 'Таупвахта.'; Ibid., s.v. 'Караул военный.' [Andreyevskiy et al., *Brockhaus and Efron Dictionary*, s.v. 'Hauptwacht.'; Ibid., s.v. 'Military guard.']

17 Palm Sunday in 1814 fell on 22 March [3 April]. Санктпетербургский Карманный Месяцеслов на лето от Рождества Христова *1814* (St. Petersburg: Императорская Академия Наук, 1814), pp.3-7. [*St. Petersburg Pocket Menologium for the Year of Our Lord 1814* (St. Petersburg: Imperial Academy of Sciences, 1814), pp.3-7.]

We departed Vilno in parade formation and I was glad that I was in the saddle again, but my enthusiasm was short lived, because after riding ten *verstas* [10.67 km] or so, my fever returned and I had to abandon my horse and place in line, trudging my way to our new quarters somehow on foot. I would walk and walk, drop down and catch my breath, and then continue on again. We arrived at our quarters rather late and I was immediately assigned back to the baggage, on which I rode for the rest of the journey to St. Petersburg.

We arrived in Strelna [in the St. Petersburg Governorate] on the 12th [24th] of October, 1814, and found the barracks and stables were inadequate, so our reserve squadron was temporarily broken up across the whole regiment and we travelled to Ropsha, eighteen *verstas* [19.2 km] from Strelna, wintering there. I was quartered with a *chukhonets*[18] and had to eat through the whole of Lent what he called '*dubina maido*' (soured milk) diluted with water and rarely anything better.[19] On the 5th [17th] June, 1815, we went on the march. Napoleon had fled the island of Elba then, but we only went as far as the city of Vilno, hanging around various villages in its vicinity for three weeks or more, and then returned to Strelna.

From 1815 to 1821, we occupied Strelna and the villages around Ropsha. In that year began dressage drills. Our squadron commander was Colonel Zaborinskiy and the regimental commander was Major General Anton Stepanovich Chalikov. I took to riding very well and came to love it, becoming proficient in the saddle.

Colonel Zaborinskiy transferred to the regular army to command a regiment. He was a fair and kindly commander for us, but in his place was assigned Colonel Kalchevskiy, who liked to drink but did not like drunks, though he did not command us for long and soon retired. He was replaced by Captain Ivan Ivanovich Kizmer. On writing this name, the pen fell out of my hand. That man was strict beyond measure. We had no senior sergeant major and his duties were being performed by Corporal Borokh, for whom Kizmer had no affection and wanted to replace with the junior Sergeant Major Gorin from the *Leib*-Squadron.[20] Under the two of them, we began to bear a heavy burden, but the world is not ours to create. For three years we were seething with anger, never completing a marching

---

18   A Karelian Finn, especially in the region of St. Petersburg. The term is now archaic and derogatory.

19   'Maido' is the Karelian form of 'maito', Finnish for milk, while 'dubina' bears a resemblance to 'dubin' a club or cudgel. This could be a euphemism for buttermilk after churning. A common name in Finland for soured or cultured milk as a beverage, such as buttermilk, is 'piimä'. Михаил Георгиевский ed., *Русско-Карельский Словарь* (St. Petersburg: Типография В. Д. Смирнова, 1908), s.v. 'молоко – майдо.'; Ibid., s.v. 'дубина – дубин.' [Mikhail Georgiyevskiy ed., *Russo-Karelian Dictionary* (St. Petersburg: V. D. Smirnov Press, 1908), s.v. 'moloko – maydo,'; Ibid., s.v. 'dubina – dubin.']

20   The most senior squadron in the regiment, nominally commanded by the regimental chief. The chief of the Guard Uhlans from 1803 to 1831 was the Tsesarevich Constantine Pavlovich. Павел Бобровский, *История Лейб-Гвардии Уланского Ея Величества Александры Феодоровны Полка*, (St. Petersburg: Экспедиция Заготовления Государственных Бумаг, 1903), Vol. 1, pp.xxi-xxiii.[Pavel Bobrovskiy, *History of the Leib-Guard Uhlan Regiment of Her Majesty Alexandra Feodorovna*, (St. Petersburg: Expedition for Storing State Papers, 1903), Vol. 1, pp.xxi-xxiii.]

or riding drill without someone being caned. The next two years were easier only because there were many inquiries about desertions – for example, thirty men ran off in one night – and from such circumstances it could be observed how our leadership managed us, so we were relieved of our brutal conditions for two years. The higher authorities probably paid close attention to Kizmer and forbade him from abusing the lower ranks from that point onward.

In 1819, I was made a non-commissioned officer, and the next day we under-officers were ordered to ride in an open-air riding hall. Colonel Kizmer ordered through Sergeant Major Gorin that I be given a horse which would not suit any soldier and demanded the impossible from me. The price for my galloon[21] was heavy, ah, so heavy.

In 1821, the Guard went on the march, or rather, for a stroll.[22] We reached only as far as Trakai in the province of Vilno, paused for some reason or other, and then returned to St. Petersburg. I was in charge of quarters for the squadron as we moved here and there, and I was worked hard during these manoeuvres.

After arriving in Strelna in 1821, we were assembled close together, with up to six men quartered on one road. I beseeched my commander, Colonel Kizmer for a three month home leave. When I was allowed to set out, I was swindled at every post I ever hired a ride, but thanks to God I arrived safely in Belyov. I visited my sister, who did not imagine she would see me again. The next day, we hired a troika and went to visit our mother in Odoyev, but before we reached home, I sent my sister on foot and then went to my brother-in-law in order to hire horses for the way to Tula. He did not recognize me and I rode off again as if we could not agree on a price. When I rode past my home, I rang the hand bell and my sister came out, not recognizing me at first, and asked: 'isn't Ivanyushka coming to visit?' Mother, following her, added: 'where is he?' I pulled over to the end of the lane and walked to the gate. I was a fine young fellow dressed in a new Guard uniform with broad golden galloon and gilded buttons with eagles embossed on them. Our joy was tremendous!

My older brother Ivan, three days before I arrived, also returned from the Caucasus where he worked as a sutler. He brought home many guests on his journey, such as a massive samovar that was boiling away on the table and an arrangement of different vodkas and hors d'oeuvres. The next day, I walked with my brother into town. As we went, friends and acquaintances continuously stopped, talked amongst themselves, and nodded to each other; what a marvel I had become!

21 Non-commissioned officers were distinguished from privates by tape of metal thread (gold or silver to match their regiment's buttons) along the edges of their collar and sleeve cuffs. Viskovatov, *Historical Description of Dress and Armament*, Vol. 11, pp.113-117.

22 Disturbances in Italy during the Congress of Laibach saw the Russian Army briefly mobilized for a campaign in 1821, but was called off before crossing the frontier. Bobrovskiy, *History of the Leib-Guard Uhlan Regiment*, Vol. 1, pp.329-330.

I stayed at home for two months and my stay was very fine, then I left with my sister for Belyov and became very ill there. I stayed with her and for a long time I made no improvement in my health. I was terribly weak for that time, but little by little I did recover. I rode back to Odoyev to say goodbye to my mother and the rest of the family. My mother then was very ill. I began to talk to my brother, for whose sake I joined the service, and ask him to give me some money for the road and, despite the fact that he recently brought back from the Caucasus over a thousand rubles, he only gave me ten paper rubles. So sad was I to be taken as a conscript, but that moment was a hundred times more dreadful. I cried and said 'So that's how I'll go back into the army, dear brother!' Mother gave me twenty-five rubles, my sister gave another twenty-five, and I said goodbye to everyone – to my mother it was forever.

When I returned to my terrible commander Colonel Kizmer, he said to me: 'you must be stuffed full of dumplings'. As he saw it, he had done me a great favour. The next day, I took a horse which had only been led about on a rope and never ridden and began to break it in properly. It needed a lot of work, but after a year I rode it while serving as an orderly of the divisional commander and received the thanks of Colonel Kizmer, seemingly the first to do so. The farther I rode, the better my horse became, and little by little commanding it became instinctual. I later rode it while acting as an orderly to the sovereign Emperor Alexander Pavlovich.

I should say that I was a good fencer. Each year we went to St. Petersburg to be inspected by the Emperor with a whole corps of fencers and fought in the Mikhaylovskiy Manège. A platform was constructed for the purpose and we were assigned to create pairs of opponents. The fencing instructor was Captain Valville, a Frenchman.[23] When we came into position and the Sovereign ordered us to begin, Valville commanded 'en garde' and we began to duel. The Sovereign ordered the instructor to present some of us, especially the best, and I was among them. We fenced for three years and each year I received the ten ruble prize. Shortly after, Colonel Kizmer was transferred to the regular army as a regimental commander and his place as squadron commander was filled by Prince Bagration (second in seniority).[24]

---

23   Alexandre Valville, fencing instructor to the Guard's cavalry and author of *Traité sur la Contre-Pointe (1817)*. Alexandre Valville, *Traité sur la Contre-Pointe* (St. Petersburg: Типография Карла Краия, 1817), pp.42-44. [Alexandre Valville, *Treatise on the Counterpoint* (St. Petersburg: Press of Karl Kray, 1817), pp.42-44.]

24   Ivan Ivanovich Kizmer became commander of Fieldmarshal Wittgenstein's (Mariupol) Hussar Regiment on 10 [22] January, 1826. He was replaced as a squadron commander by Prince Dmitriy Georgievich Bagration-Imeretinskiy, who was then a *Rittmeister* (Captain). The 'First' Bagration in the regiment was his older brother, Prince Alexander Geogievich. The Imeretinskiy branch was far removed genealogically from the famous general Pyotr Bagration who had commanded the Second Western Army in 1812 until his mortal wounding at Borodino. Bobrovskiy, *History of the Leib-Guard Uhlan Regiment*, appendix to Vol. 2, pp.301-307.

Emperor Nicholas I of Russia (Reigned 1825-1855). Franz Krüger, 1852, oil on canvas, St. Petersburg, State Hermitage Museum.

For the coronation of Nicholas Pavlovich, two whole squadrons from each regiment were ordered to be present in Moscow. I was assigned to the second squadron under Colonel Tornau. In the order to our regiment it was written that all the men of the coronation detachment were to be mounted on their own horses but in practice this was not carried out. Prince Bagration, my former squadron commander, kept my horse and I was given another shoddy mount, but it was not possible to complain. When we departed for Moscow and had reached the town of Volochyok, where the Grand Prince Michael Pavlovich ordered from each squadron an NCO to take as an orderly and a private to ferry messages, Colonel Tornau ordered every non-commissioned officer to ride his own horse and tested each as equally as possible. The examination was somewhat complex and not easy. He chose me to be one of the orderlies but mounted me on what you might call an old nag. Our regiment was styled 'consolidated' because we were joined by two squadrons of dragoons and I was told to present myself by saying 'To Your Imperial Majesty from the *Leib*-Guard's First Consolidated Light Cavalry Regiment, from the squadron of Colonel Tornau, I am sent as an orderly'. One had to say all of this without any pause or hesitation. With us was the handsome Lieutenant Bryanchaninov who was extraordinarily mounted, and he was delighted to order the whole riding hall routine from us when we were presented to the Grand Prince, personally leading us through the manoeuvres. Michael Pavlovich was very pleased with our riding and ordered that ten rubles be awarded to each NCO, and five to each private.

To be continued.[25]

---

25 No further chapters to 'The Recollections of Ivan Menshoy' were ever published by *Russian Antiquity.*

Stories of the Campaigns of 1812 and 1813 from an Ensign of the Saint-Petersburg Militia, by Rafail Mikhaylovich Zotov

I

The year 1812! What a magical phrase! What tremendous memories! Twenty-four years have passed since that era and its gigantic events still seem like figments of our imaginations from last night's dream, which we are still dreaming with all force and liveliness – and we try to recall every smallest detail of it – and when we have found them in our memory we rush with delight to recall it all to our family and friends. It has been a quarter of a century since and almost half of the present generation took an active role in that magnificent drama; the rest have disappeared from the scene and only occasionally are their names repeated in their circles of friends and family. Another quarter of a century will pass and perhaps not one of the original actors will still remain. However, the memories of their deeds will be stronger than the countless monuments erected by human vanity.

The story of the most insignificant member[1] of that great endeavour of the time naturally cannot be entertaining in either historical, military, or literary terms, but it can serve to an observer as an image of the great spirit of the times which animated Russia in every corner and through all the classes. And for an aging participant of those skirmishes, this narrative will refresh and rejuvenate all those former, glorious and valiant events. And if the young moustache of a blooming warrior should curl with disappointment on reading the words 'ensign' and 'militia', then a grey veteran will with true and sincere pleasure read on for a few

---

1 Zotov's note: 'Baron Steinheil, shortly after the campaign, published historical notes on the St. Petersburg Militia. Having described all the battles in which it participated, he even preserved the names of all the officers which distinguished themselves. In Part 2 on pages 173 and 174, I, an insignificant ensign, am recorded, and I, having never personally known the author or even seeing him, give him now after 20 years all of my sincere thanks for his very flattering review of me, of which I am still proud'.

pages and be reminded of the famous names of Wittgenstein, Klyastitsy, Polotsk, and Berezina.

As a precocious and diligent student, I had already graduated from my course at 16 and with a title important to me (Student of the 14th Class) joined the civil service.[2] Who in their youth has not dreamed of the beauty of a military uniform, of the virtuous camp life and of glorious feats in battle? And so? I must confess that such a dream never came to my mind. I was addicted to poetry and astronomy, in both my dreams and in my real eyes I only saw the ellipses of comets and solemn odes, the fires of my youth were filled with daydreaming of all the visible planets, all the vastness of the universe, residents of various shapes, properties and longevity – and yet at the same time I poured sweat over iambic tetrameter. I imagined that I would become the next Newton or Derzhavin,[3] and now after 25 years and with bitter but humble self-awareness I see that neither of those two passions has brought me any benefit or fame. Like millions of dreamers, I saw that I was in a very confined sphere of mediocrity and insignificance.

Not even six months had passed since my entry into service when news broke of Napoleon's invasion of Russia, and all of Europe, led by Napoleon, jumped across Russia's far corners like an electric spark and terrified the hearts of all Russians. The famous rescript to Count Saltykov, the order to the army, and manifesto on the defence of the fatherland created such an impact and revived such impulses of love for the fatherland, that no pen can describe it. One witness remembers these great and sacred days, when both life and wealth were esteemed not as personal property, but as the property of the fatherland, such was the outrage at the audacious invasion of the foreigners. How sweet it is to remember that time of universal enthusiasm! Now such outbursts, close to frenzy, would be rebuked or even ridiculed;[4] but at the time they did not surprise anyone, since everyone felt

[margin notes, handwritten: "similar to volunteers/ finishing college before enlisting in WWII", "Is such a zeitgeist possible in our own age?", "what modern wars/events have shaped our culture? our lives?", "Is this closest to 9/11?"]

2   The 14th Class was the lowest Rank in the *Table of Ranks*, and would enable Zotov to enlist in the army as an ensign or cornet or into the civil service as a collegiate registrar or equivalent post. Civil servants volunteering for the militia were able to gain the military equivalent of their present rank, vacancies permitting. Shepelyov, *Titles, Uniforms and Orders*, pp.117-118.; *Ibid.*, p.154.; Владимир Штейнгейль, *Записки Касательно Составления и Самого Похода Санктпетербургского Ополчения против Врагов Отечества в 1812 и 1813 годах*, (St. Petersburg: Типография В. Плавильщикова, 1814), Vol. 1, pp.41-42. [Vladimir Steinheil, *Notes Regarding the Creation and Campaigning of the St. Petersburg Militia against the Enemies of the Fatherland in 1812 and 1813*, (St. Petersburg: Press of V. Plavil'shchikov, 1814), Vol. 1, pp.41-42.]

3   Gavriil Romanovich Derzhavin was perhaps the most celebrated Russian poet of the 18th Century but also held such posts as Governor of Olonets and Tambov, State-Secretary, Senator, President of the Commerce Collegium, and Minister of Justice. Andreyevskiy et al., *Brockhaus and Efron Dictionary*, s.v. 'Державин, Гавриил Романович.' [Andreyevskiy et al., *Brockhaus and Efron Dictionary*, s.v. 'Derzhavin, Gavriil Romanovich.'

4   Zotov's note: 'For example, in a theatre during the performance of the drama *Love for the Fatherland*, when all the actors brought out their possessions to sacrifice them to the country, one of the spectators threw his wallet onto the stage and shouted 'there's the last of my money!"

Emperor Napoleon I of France (Reigned 1804-1814, again in 1815). Jacques-Louis David, 1812, oil on canvas, Washington D.C., National Gallery of Art.

the same way. On the streets, in every community, in the family circle, there was no other topic of conversation but the people's war. All the town gossip, quarrels and feuds fell silent, as patriotism reconciled them all. Whole crowds of people stood in the streets and squares, eagerly waiting for the couriers from the army. Every communique was consumed, reread a thousand times over, and memorized; the names of heroes were echoed by a thousand voices. The first victory made Count Wittgenstein a favourite of the Russian people. The excitement produced by the news of the Battle of Klyastitsy is impossible to describe.[5] From that moment, everyone demanded news of Count Wittgenstein daily, so universally adored had his name become. Indeed fate had placed him in the most favourable position. While the main army was retreating daily, he alone managed to repel the enemy and alone became the hard breast that would not let them past the Dvina. That resistance, constituting the general character of the Russian people, struck straight to the heart and in that moment was valued as his greatest merit.

At this time came the manifesto on the establishment of the militia.[6] Everyone was excited and rushed to arms. The Sovereign demanded four souls be taken for every hundred, but the nobility of St. Petersburg announced they would give ten per hundred and supply them with weapons, provisions, and salaries for the first months. All the provinces enthusiastically followed this noble example. Everywhere flocked crowds of warriors, combined into *druzhinas*. Count Kutuzov was chosen as the commander of the St. Petersburg militia and perhaps this very choice, as the voice of the people to entrust him as our leader, illustrated to the wise that this hero would become the saviour of Russia.[7]

---

5   The Battle at Klyastitsy was fought from 18 [30] July to 20 July [1 August], 1812. 'Донесение П. Х. Виттенштейна от 21 Июля (2 Августа) 1812,' *Интернет-проект «1812 год»*, last modified 2005. ['Report from P. Kh. Wittgenstein from the 21 July (2 August) 1812,' *Internet Project '1812'*, last modified 2005.] http://www.museum.ru/museum/1812/war/news_rus/izv022.html.

6   The manifesto on forming a national militia and its organization was issued on 18 [30] July, 1812. *Complete Collection of Laws*, Collection 1, Vol. 32, pp.397-398. No. 25,188.

7   Mikhail Illarionovich Golenishchev-Kutuzov had an uneasy relationship with the Emperor Alexander. From the position of commander-in-chief of the ill-fated Russian forces at Austerlitz, he fell to corps commander in 1809 to participate in the Russo-Turkish War of 1806-1812, then left the field to become General-Governor of Lithuania, rejoined again with the rank of General of Infantry and the distinction of Count to assume full command of the Army of the Danube and brought an end to that war finally on 16 [28] May, 1812. He was recalled to St. Petersburg and became responsible for the city's defense and the raising of the Militia on 12 [24] June. After the Battle of Smolensk, the personalities and strategies of Barclay de Tolly and Bagration, commanders of the 1st and 2nd Western Armies, were threatening to split the officer corps and imperil the army, so Alexander was compelled to appoint a third leader to supersede and unify them. By popular choice, he conceded to appoint Kutuzov to that task, making him commander-in-chief of the combined armies on 5 [17] August. He was promoted to General Field Marshal on 31 August [12 September], just one day before the decision at Fili to abandon Moscow to the French. He died on 16 [28] April, 1813, having seen Napoleon driven out of Russia. Andreyevskiy et al., *Brockhaus and Efron Dictionary*, s.v. 'Кутузов-Голенищев.'; Любомир Бескровный ed., *М. И. Кутузов: Сборник Документов* (Moscow: Военное Издательство Министерства Обороны СССР, 1954), Vol.

Field Marshal Mikhail Golenishchev-Kutuzov. Commander of St. Petersburg's Defence and Commander-in-Chief of the Combined Armies. George Dawe, 1829, oil on canvas, St. Petersburg, State Hermitage Museum.

Opposite New Holland Island in the home of Baron Rall, the Committee for the Militia opened their meeting. Everyone asking to be admitted into the ranks of that force was received there. I stood among this crowd wishing to join with my magnificent rank of XIV and the vivid imagination of a 16-year-old youth who strutted about with the firm belief that he would capture Napoleon himself. While all the civil officials were enlisted, their positions were occupied until their return and they received their wages for them. Despite how favourable the conditions seem, I can safely assert that no one was guided by self-interest. And I truthfully least of all, since I then received (guiltily) 150 rubles a year. We were given half a year's salary (180 rubles) for outfitting our uniforms and (imagine my delight!) several days later I was among an audience in golden epaulettes and a bicorne with a plume. Then all manner of action began to boil over rapidly. Who today could believe that some 14,000 men, just torn from the plough and with no concept of military service, were trained in all the movements of drill in only five days? They might say: 'of course they learned it poorly' – No! I swear that not only did they all march at the quick step very smoothly (though the ceremonial march was postponed to a more convenient time), not only did they perform all the movements of the musket smoothly and fired by command and without commands, but they even formed columns and squares by their various platoons.[8] And all in five days or rather five days and nights, since in the long summer hours we through the night almost never left the Izmaylovskiy parade grounds on which we trained. The Commandant Bashutskiy was our instructor and our rapid progress surpassed all expectations. Only with the Russian people can such wonders be worked.

On the 30th of August [11th of September], St. Alexander's Day, the whole of Petersburg was enraptured by the news of the Battle of Borodino. In the present circumstances, it had to be considered a great victory and the general enthusiasm reached a frenzy. Only one thing seemed greatly disappointing to us: all of our friends and acquaintances that we met on that day would tell us militiamen 'you're not needed any longer! No more! After Borodino, the French will flee from Russia!'

4, Part 1, p.3.; *Ibid.*, p.71.; *Ibid.* pp.193-221. [Andreyevskiy et al., *Brockhaus and Efron Dictionary*, s.v. 'Kutuzov-Golenishchev.'; Lyubomir Beskrovnyy ed., *M. I. Kutuzov: Collection of Documents* (Moscow: Military Publishing of the Ministry of Defense of the USSR, 1954) , Vol. 4, Part 1 p.3.; *Ibid.*, p.71.; *Ibid.*, p.193-221].

8   The quick step was defined as 120 paces per minute by order of the Emperor, conveyed to Constantine Pavlovich in a letter by General-Adjutant Pyotr Petrovich Dolgorukov on 22 February [6 March], 1803. The ordinary step was set at 75. Each pace was defined as having a length of one *arshin* [71.12 cm]. Д. А. Скалон and Н. П. Михневич eds., *Столетие Военного Министерства 1802-1902* (St. Petersburg: Тип. 'Бережливость', 1903), Part 4, Section 1, Book 2, Vol. 3, p.185.; *Воинской Устав о Пехотной Службе*, (St. Petersburg: Типография Ученого Комитета по Артиллерийской Части, 1811), Vol 1, pp.18-19. [D. A. Skalon and N. P. Mikhnevich eds., *Centenary of the War Ministry 1802-1902*, (St. Petersburg: 'Prudence' Press, 1903), Part 4, Section 1, Book 2, Vol. 3, p.185.; *Military Regulations on the Infantry Service*, (St. Petersburg: Press of the Scientific Committee of the Artillery Department, 1811), Vol. 1, pp.18-19].

No matter how joyous was the thought of such an immediate expulsion of the enemy from the country, we felt great sorrow at the prospect of throwing away the brilliant uniform and returning to the humble clerical ranks without even once drawing the sword from its scabbard or smelling gunpowder. I also remember how on that day I visited the Nevskiy Monastery for mass and despite the fact that they were expecting the immediate arrival of the Imperial Family, I was admitted into the church without hindrance.[9] What a tremendous privilege these golden epaulettes afforded me! The officer on guard remarked to me rightfully that on such a day it was not wise to be in my frock coat (though my tailcoat was not finished), and that I should not have tied my cravat with the bow in the front, but in the heat of the moment, no one besides him paid any attention to me. Some friends admired my attire. In the evening at the Maliy Theatre they gave the first performance of a new drama, *The Universal Militia*, which was such a success and so enthralling that everyone had seen at least one performance.[10]

The next day, we thoroughly learned again all the ceremonial manoeuvres and on the 1st [13th] of September, we passed through the St. Isaac's and Palace Squares. There, the Metropolitan, having served the litany, consecrated our banner,[11] and sprinkled us with holy water before the Emperor made a tour of our ranks. Then we marched passed him at the quick step by half-platoons, filling the air with a sincere and joyful 'ura!' On the 3rd [15th] of the month, the first half the militia had already departed on campaign, and on the 5th [17th], our column joined them.

Even now, that day is fresh in my memory. On the vast Semyonovskiy parade ground we assembled. The day was warm and beautiful and countless people gathered. Already we fell silent since nothing needed to be said, because after Borodino, the Russian Army continued to retreat; therefore our armed force which seemed very strong on the city square, had the appearance of certain importance. At nine in the morning, the Emperor came to us accompanied by the Minister of War[12] and the English ambassador.[13] The Emperor himself ordered us to form columns

[margin: Question 1.]

9   The Saint Alexandr Nevskiy Monastery in St. Petersburg.

10 The theatre is now known as the A.S. Pushkin Russian State Academy Drama Theatre. Иван Пушкарев, *Описание Санктпетербурга и Уездных Городов С. Петербургской Губернии* (St. Petersburg: Типография Н. Греча, 1839), Vol. 3, pp.122-123. [Ivan Pushkarev, *Description of St. Petersburg and the County Capitals of the St. Petersburg Governorate* (St. Petetersburg: Press of N. Grech, 1839), Vol. 3, pp.122-123.]

11 Zotov's note: 'It was from white cloth, on which the eight-pointed cross was emblazoned with the [Church Slavonic] inscription on both sides: 'In This Sign You Will Conquer'.'

12 Prince Aleksey Ivanovich Gorchakov acted as Minister of the Land Forces from 24 August [5 September], 1812 to 12 [24] December, 1815. Д. А. Скалон and Н. А. Данилов eds., *Столетие Военного Министерства 1802-1902* (St. Petersburg: Типография П. Ф. Пантелеева, 1902), Part 1, Vol. 1, pp.211-225. [D. A. Skalon and N. A. Danilov eds., *Centenary of the War Ministry 1802-1902* (St. Petersburg: Press of P. F. Panteleyev, 1902), Part 1, Vol. 1, pp.211-225].

13 William, Viscount Cathcart (later Earl Cathcart) was the United Kingdom's ambassador to Russia from 13 [25] July, 1812 until 11 [23] May, 1820. Joseph Haydn, *The Book of Dignities Containing the Rolls of the*

and stand at prayer,[14] dismounted from his horse and approached the Metropolitan who stood waiting in the company of his many clergymen, took a cross for around his neck, and then the prayer for intercession began. When the protodeacon[15] proclaimed 'again and again, bending our knees, [putting them to the ground, let us pray to the Lord,]' The Sovereign, the clergy and all the columns of the militia knelt down to warmly and lovingly beg for success in righteous battle.

When the prayer was finished, the Metropolitan gave a short speech to the soldiers and blessed them with the icon of Saint Alexander Nevskiy and then handed it to General Begichev,[16] who was in command of all the men assembled on that day. Everyone shouted in unison that we were happy to die for the faith and the Tsar![17] The Metropolitan walked through the ranks and sprinkled them with holy water and then the Sovereign Emperor himself, mounting his horse again, commanded us to shoulder arms and march. Everyone departed past him with a ceaseless cry of '*ura!*' When all the platoons had passed, he caught up with them and while standing gave a short but powerful speech before them, in which he expressed his complete confidence and hope in the loyalty and bravery of the warriors. The cheers were ceaseless; everyone was overwhelmed with joy. Few noticed that the Emperor was in a mournful mood, and that even when kneeling to pray, his eyes were tearful. None of us at the time knew just what a disaster had befallen Russia. The Emperor alone knew of the terrible event but he would not risk a timeless gloom on the serving army and people, so he concealed this national tragedy for several days. Moscow was already in the hands of the enemy![18]

Is it any wonder that the Emperor, not being able to foresee how this terrible war would end, grieved in his soul like a father over the fates of millions of his children, entrusted to him by Providence? Is it any wonder that having sent the last batch of soldiers into battle, he knelt before the Almighty and shed tears over the fates that befell the thousands of victims fallen or soon to fall for the salvation of the fatherland? Great were the tears of the monarch, profound were those

---

Official Personages of the British Empire (London: Long, Brown, Green and Longmans, 1851), p.81.

14 From order arms, the soldier rested his weapon into the crook of his left arm without moving the butt by his right foot and then removes his headgear and lays it into his open left hand. His right hand is then free to make the sign of the cross during the service. *Military Regulations of 1811*, p.31.

15 The first and leading deacon of a diocese, holding his post typically at the diocesan cathedral. Andreyevskiy et al., *Brockhaus and Efron Dictionary*, s.v. 'Протодиакон.' [Andreyevskiy et al., *Brockhaus and Efron Dictionary*, s.v. 'Protodeacon'].

16 The first column of the militia was under the command of Privy Councillor (rank III) and Senator Alexander Alexandrovich Bibikov and the second under Major General (rank IV) Ivan Matveyevich Begichev. Steinheil, *Notes Regarding the St. Petersburg Militia*, Vol. 1, pp.52-53.

17 'For the faith and the Tsar' was a slogan embroidered on the banners or stamped onto the brass cap badges of several militia units raised during 1812, including the St. Petersburg levy. Viskovatov, *Historical Description of Dress and Armament*, Vol. 18, pp.81-127.

18 Napoleon entered Moscow on 2 [14] September, 1812 and did not leave until 6 [18] October. Ward et al, *Cambridge Modern History*, Vol. 9, pp.496-498.

high passions which inspired him in that moment! He saw the universal desire to prepare for self-sacrifice and trusted Providence with the fate of the people, so strong was the love of our sovereign.

Nearly the whole city accompanied us as we left in the direction of the Moscow Gates, and we spent the night in the village of Pulkovo, resting our heads in our hands. This first overnight encampment offered so many new sights and experiences for everyone. Who could know then that we would march so far away and return again? Hunched down in the corner of a peasant's log house, each of us spent ten minutes to think and dream about the forthcoming stage, the conclusion of which no one could foretell. I say ten minutes because each man inevitably closed his eyes from fatigue. The next day, we reached Gatchina and stayed there for the night. This change was quite heavy for novices who might take a walk to Krestovskiy Island and imagine they had strayed too far. Here I spent two nights in the smoky hut of a *chukhonets*[19] for the first time. In the following days we were treated to the same comforts, especially in Lithuania, but for the first time it was very unpleasant: lying on a bench and not daring to climb up a level for fear of being choked by the haze of smoke clinging to the ceiling and being unable to venture outside due to torrential rains.

The first movement from Gatchina was the most severe for the *druzhina* to which I belonged (the 14th).[20] Each day it was impossible to encamp the whole column along the main road, so a portion would have to spread out up to five *verstas* [5.33 km] and the next day they would sometimes lag 10 *verstas* [10.67 km] or more from the more fortunate troops. That was the case during that movement: my smoky house in Gatchina was five *verstas* from the main road, the march to the next night's camp was 32 *verstas* [34.14 km] and then we needed to depart from the road for another five to reach our new quarters, totalling 42 [44.81 km]. This little adventure forced me to perform even greater feats. Stopping to eat usually lasted two hours. Being bored to wait so long, I chose to go on ahead with a comrade, hoping to reach my night's rest an hour earlier and have time to relax before the others. Along the way we came upon another *druzhina* which had already halted, and found some acquaintances. We had a very pleasant conversation about our future exploits and eventually evening fell. The quarters-officers of different *druzhina*s had then arrived and I asked the first one about a place

---

19   A Karelian Finn, especially in the region of St. Petersburg. The term is now archaic and derogatory.

20   The St. Petersburg Militia's infantry originally consisted of 15 units roughly equal to a battalion, ideally containing 800 private soldiers each, but referred to as a 'дружина' (druzhina), evoking a medieval band of free warriors. Likewise, its subdivision was not called a company, but a 'сотня' (sotnya) meaning a century or a hundred men, although it was twice the size of its namesake. Four *sotnya*s to a *druzhina* mirrored the structure of a regular army battalion and when three *druzhina*s were grouped into a 'brigade', they were essentially a large regiment. The 14th *Druzhina* was commanded by a Colonel Chernov. Beskrovnyy, *M. I. Kutuzov: Collection of Documents*, pp.57-63.; Steinheil, *Notes Regarding the St. Petersburg Militia*, Vol. 1, pp.51-53; *Military Regulations of 1811*, p.1.

to sleep. Learning and memorizing the name of the village (Podgorye), I happily hiked on ahead. It soon became dark and my friend became badly exhausted. I was still resolved, and had a good laugh at one of his fictions, namely that he believed you could completely avert fatigue so long as you rested as often as possible; therefore he would run a quarter of a *versta* [266.7 m] ahead, sit down and wait until I caught up to him walking at a steady pace. As it turned out, he was wrong and had spent himself. While passing through a village at the time in which one *druzhina* had stopped for the night, he found another friend and decided to spend the night with him, and asked me to inform our commander. So I went off alone, and all night I asked every minute: how far was the village to which the officer directed me? Another two *versta*s [2.13 km], I was told, and I would gather the strength and continue at a brisk pace. How far was two *versta*s? But I had arrived!

But what's this? What terrible misfortune had struck me? I had in truth come to Podgorye, but this was Greater Podgorye and was arranged for the quartering of – I believe – the 6th *Druzhina*, whereas we were meant to sleep in Lesser Podgorye, which was behind me and four *versta*s [4.27 km] off the main road. My heart sank and I slowly walked back. Little by little I lost my strength and could barely move my feet, hoping that the day's 50 *versta*s [53.34 km] had already been surpassed. I regularly passed people on the road back and asked them which way to turn off the road, and most answered me in the folksy way: 'couldn't say'. And with every answer, my steps became slower. At last I saw some kind of intersection and at the bend was one of our non-commissioned officers serving as quarters-officer. This bolstered my courage and I walked with him along that overgrown country road. However, I soon felt that the cheer in my mind was no substitute for my legs. My strength was completely and decisively exhausted. A few minutes later, I was silent and withholding my shame for as long as I could, but it finally defeated me. I said to the NCO that I could not continue. He tried to persuade me that it was not much farther, showing the flickering of fires, but I would not have it – I was completely immobile. Even still I remember that unfathomable aching. Several times I tried with all my willpower to force myself to stand up, but I could not do it for long. In desperation, I sprawled out on the grass and told him that he could go on to the village and I would stay the night where I lay. The NCO, fearing the captain, did not listen to me and decided to wait until I was rested. For half an hour I lay motionless, until finally the night cold began to fall upon me and I tried moving my legs to happily discover that they would obey me again. With the help of the NCO, I climbed up and swayed for a moment where I stood, then I slowly walked toward the village, holding his hand to steady me.

Somehow, I managed to arrive at the promised village and somehow clambered up the stairs into captain's cabin. I saw that a corner had been prepared with straw for us and rushed for it without saying a word to anyone. Everyone showered me with questions. Lying down, I told them about my stupid mistake and asked the captain to record me on his report of casualties so that in the morning I could ride with the baggage train. 'Oh nonsense, brother', said the captain, 'go to sleep, rest up, and get up refreshed!' I was sure that what he said was impossible, but I did not have the strength to argue. Refusing any meal, I was soon snoring in just a few minutes.

A drumbeat and the captain's voice woke me up at dawn. I jumped up and, to my amazement, not even the tiniest trace of my former fatigue remained. My strength and vitality were restored. Laziness held my arms down and my mouth agape in a yawn, but cold water quickly banished it and I was ready to march again. Taking the previous day as a lesson, I never again ventured far ahead and humbly followed my platoon, recovering on the march those hours which were stolen from me by my early awakening until the first stop. Do not think, dear readers, that the phrase 'recovering on the march' is some figure of speech or witticism. No, I swear to you that after a hard journey without proper sleep and an early rising, and when taking to the road again straight away, then while marching in the ranks of your platoon, constantly falling asleep on the move, you will dream, stumble and wake up, and then dream again.[21] Ask the frontline officers of the army; they will verify it happens often.

The second rest was taken in Luga and nothing noteworthy happened. The third, however, was memorable. It was at the Feofilov Hermitage. It was there that we first heard that the French had taken Moscow! I could not hope to convey to the reader what a horrible effect was made on us by this news. The feeling is inexpressible. An absolute gloom covered us. We looked to the future now with such a sad indifference and silent anguish. It seemed as if everything was lost, that the war had no purpose anymore except the last, desperate effort of a dying man or the final destruction of those Russians remaining. Until that point, we had dreamed of glorious feats, but now the whole scope of our imagination was limited to death. Our noisy conversations at night came to an end and we now silently agreed together, shaking each other's hands and nodding. Silently we wiped the tears from our eyes. Most of all, we were afraid of a humiliating peace – to us, death seemed preferable by far.

With these painful feelings, we resumed the march. Nothing else remarkable happened until Velikiy Luki. We were ordered to remain there for two days and everyone visited the baths, mended our equipment and prepared for a long bivouac. It was here that we heard for the first time about the French marauders, from which nearly the entire city had fled by St. Elijah's Friday,[22] and it was here that we found the most cordial and selfless residents receiving us. They completely refused to accept money from us. I needed to buy a few *funt*s of sugar. The merchant

---

21   Incidents of soldiers falling asleep on the march without stumbling are known in many armies and eras.

22   St. Elijah's (Ilyin's) Day was 20 July (1 August), and fell on a Saturday in 1812, making Ilyin's Friday the 19 [31]. *Месяцеслов с Росписью Чиновных Особ, или Общий Штат Российской Империи на Лето от Рождества Христова 1812* (St. Petersburg: Императорская Академия Наук, 1812), Vol. 1, p.ix. [*Menologium with a List of the Ranking Individuals or a General State of the Russian Empire in the Year of Our Lord 1812* (St. Petersburg: Imperial Academy of Sciences, 1812), Vol. 1, p.ix].

weighted it and became very upset when I asked how much it would cost. 'Why, friend, would I take anything of yours for free?'

He replied: 'because you are our protectors, our saviours!'

I said to him: 'but if all of your protectors come to take your goods without paying, you'll have nothing left'.

'But, my good man, no one is left in town; we have much and we decided before you came that we would not charge you anything. I am lucky that you came and I am glad to serve a little to Your Nobleness!'[23] I took his goods and hurried to my quarters to tell everyone about the patriotic selflessness of the whole town, but my news was already old. Many before me had experienced the same generosity and to the honour of the militia it must be said that no one in those two days asked for anything in excess to stock up and were content with the cordial entertainment of the residents.

On the 26th of September [8th October], we departed from that veritable El Dorado and for a long, long time we went without beds and roofs, we did not sit at any tables, we never undressed, nor did we have enough to eat and drink. Until then, we were accustomed to sleeping in village homes every evening after a day's march. On that day, we found our quarters in a vast field with a lake on one side and a dense forest on the other. 'Where is our lodging?' we asked the quarters-officers.

'But here they are', they replied and pointed around the field bristling with stakes. Those stakes demarcated the camping areas between the different *druzhinas*. As soon as the column broke up into its components, we were immediately sent into the forest by platoons, pounding and crackling and snapping limbs as we went. Fires were built, pots were hung for cooking, provisions were brought out, and thanks to the dexterity of the Russian, in an hour, hundreds of wicker huts adorned the empty field. In another hour, the whole camp slept the sleep of heroic warriors. Some did not sleep well, waking frequently and crawling out of their huts to warm by the fires with the assistance of the sentries. For me, the flexibility of youth and never having lived a sybaritic lifestyle, I fell asleep quickly and did not stir until morning. The tireless drum raised us all at dawn. We leapt up, ran to the lake to wash, crossed ourselves, put on and tightened up our backpacks and, upon a second drumbeat, we resumed our march.

That evening, we made camp in the same fashion, but on the third night we were pampered again. The first Lithuanian town we reached, Nevel,[24] took us under their roofs for a night and day's rest. But what a brutal contrast did we find in the

---

23 'Ваше Благородие' (Vashe Blagorodiye), literally 'Your Nobleness', was the formal address for the lowest ranking nobility, grades XIV to IX (ensign to captain). Shepelyov, *Titles, Uniforms and Orders*, pp.28-29.

24 Nevel was encompassed by the Polish-Lithuanian Commonwealth before the partition of 1772. After 1802, it fell within the Vitebsk Governorate. Today it lies in the Pskov Oblast of the Russian Federation. *Complete Collection of Laws*, Collection 1, Vol. 27, pp.59-60. No. 20,162.; *Pocket Postal Atlas of the Russian Empire*, p.6.

sentiments and reception of our hosts! It is true that they did not demand money from us, but they also gave nothing in kind. The townsfolk glanced at us and hid their provisions in their cellars and the merchants locked their shops, while the cosmopolitans – the Jews – ran around us, assuring us all of their constant devotion to Russia and bartering for the last of our money.

Departing from Nevel, we found ourselves in a new world. Our transits were already on a completely martial footing. A vanguard, patrols, lit linstocks with every artillery brigade, cavalry screens; in short, all the necessary precautions for our proximity to the enemy. But where was he? Our hearts boiled impatiently with the desire to shout at him our valiant *ura*!

On the 31st of September [12th October], we came to the settlement of Krasnopolye, washed in the River Drissa and were bivouacked in the vast meadows nearby. We stayed there for three days because the bridge over the Drissa was burned by our parties as a precaution during Count Wittgenstein's retreat. The very first night was troublesome for me. When our *druzhina* was settled into the bivouac, I was ordered to take a platoon to the nearby lake for picket duty. The lieutenant colonel, an old serviceman, in sending me, believed that I properly knew what the word 'picket' meant and what sort of ceremony took place when the officers making the rounds passed by. I thought with complete innocence that we would lie down for the night all the same at the lake or on the field. My soldiers built a fire and put together a hovel for me. I dined on buckwheat porridge, took off my sash, threw down my backpack and calmly lay down.

But even before I could fall asleep, a non-commissioned officer rushed up to me and shouted 'Your Nobleness! The rounds are coming!'

'And so what?' I answered, stretching out.

'You have to receive them'.

'Well by all means', I said as I put on my forage cap and clambered out of the hut.

Suddenly I heard very impolite questions: 'Who's the guard officer!? Where is he!?' I found myself before some general, who was making the rounds personally to inspect our serviceability. 'What is the meaning of this? Where were you, sir? This is how you meet the rounds? How dare you remove your sash and backpack!' and other affectionate questions rained down on me with the gracious promise of having me arrested. I did not understand my guilt but like a Russian I kept silent. Seeing my meek fear, the general guessed that this was all Greek to me and asked me my surname and *druzhina*, and demanded that I repeat to him the instructions which I was given when I was put on picket duty. I carefully answered that I had received no instructions and thought that today's camp would be like all the previous, when we had no obligations. The general smiled, was relieved, and sent for my lieutenant colonel. The poor old man got a proper earful, but then it was over.

At that point, I spent half the night with an old NCO from the regular army learning the mysteries of military science and applied them when the next rounds passed by, personally receiving them with all the ceremonial movements. After

Senator Aleksandr Bibikov. Commander of the St. Petersburg and Novgorod Militias. George Dawe, 1828, oil on canvas, St. Petersburg, State Hermitage Museum.

that, the NCO told me that there would be no more visitors and I could sleep safely until morning, a luxury in which I indulged with a particular pleasure.

On the 4th [16th] of October, we departed from Krasnopolye over the new bridge built in that time by our militia. That was when we saw for the first time the leader of our militia, Senator Bibikov, who had departed from St. Petersburg on the 5th [17th] of September with the First Column by a different road (through Pskov and Sebezh) and only now did the two columns unite. He himself ordered us to depart on the march and was very pleased with our condition, because we took to the road, performed the different evolutions and formed columns, all with full force. During the last two days of our stay in Krasnopolye, it was pouring rain and our fashioned shelters offered poor protection against it. We were drying off and warming up at fires at all times, but this was the work of Penelope,[25] drying on the one hand and soaking on the other. The morning departure from Krasnopolye however was clear and warm.

25 In Homer's *Odyssey*, Penelope delayed choosing a suitor by first weaving a funeral shroud for her absent husband's father, but every night she would secretly unravel as much as she wove so that it was never finished. George Palmer (Trans.), *The Odyssey of Homer* (Cambridge: Riverside Press, 1892), p.18.

After travelling eleven *verstas* [11.73 km], we were made to stop at a rundown tavern, performed a prayer and listened to a speech from our commanding general on the proximity of the enemy, to which we responded by shouting '*ura!*' Then we continued our march. After another six *verstas* [6.4 km] we were suddenly ordered to stop and bivouac by a lake. The October rain drenched us again and we quickly constructed our straw and wicker huts and hoped to warm and dry ourselves by the fires. But it was not to be!

The enemy was close. He should not have known of the existence of our columns or their approach, so it was not ordered to douse the fires. Things became poor very quickly. Another equal dilemma was that our baggage train remained in Krasnopolye and we had only stale black rusk for our meals, which were in the soldiers' backpacks, being softened up in the water of the lake. In a rather dampened mood we retired for the night in our huts and piled on top of them as many branches and leaves as we could to keep the rain out, and made bedding inside of much the same. As nature always had the last say, we sighed at our futility for a few minutes and then fell asleep. A new calamity woke us two hours before dawn. The rain, unceasing through the whole night, made a lake out of the whole area of our camp and the water washed away our shelters and bedding. It was the most painful feeling. The side on which I was lying curled up was submerged and soaked through and my dream was interrupted by feverish shivering which nothing could help. A profound silence fell over the camp. No one could warm up or dry off or even leave and walk around to get their blood flowing. With the rain from above and the water below climbing up our legs, nothing was possible. The rest of the night was the worst of the whole campaign. (In 1813, when we arrived in Prussia in the spring, we forged a river where it was shallow and the whole column had to walk in water up to our knees for more than a mile, yet all the while the soldiers and officers were laughing and joking. Everyone knew that by evening they would be warm, dry and have a hearty meal.) By dawn, no one needed a drumbeat to wake them, no bathing was required, as they had been washed from head to toe, and it was pointless to think about breakfast when there was nothing to eat! Everyone waited for the second drumbeat to assemble for the march like it was God's Mercy, but at the time the drum failed us and we waited in vain. A command came from headquarters: to remain in place until further instructions. That was the final blow.

An hour later, fate smiled on me. I was sent to the vanguard picket. It was on the main road where instead of water there was only mud and where one could recover their spirits. Remembering my failure on picket at Krasnopolye, I demanded instructions and was told not to admit anyone down the road without strict examination, bringing them immediately to the detachment. With a light heart from the night of suffering, I went to my post and began to knead the mud with great import and drop the point of my sword into the puddles on the side of the road. In that simple activity which entertained me and dispelled my sadness, I passed several hours. The time came to dine, and the soldiers began to consume the last remnants of the bread reserve. I shared in their modest meal and then, to help digest it, I went back to my stomping down the road. All I know is that that day was the longest in my life. I constantly glanced at my silver Walther [pocket watch] and the hands would not move forward.

Suddenly close to dusk, I saw riders galloping down the road and obviously stopped them. It turned out to be a Russian officer in the company of two Cossacks. He was very upset, both with stopping and with my questions. Instead of answering me, he asked me who ordered me to halt passers-by in the rearguard and so on. While our conversation continued, an officer of the day from the chain of posts arrived who asked all the same questions I did. Seeing that he would not make headway with us, he announced that he was riding from Count Wittgenstein to the general commanding our column with orders to immediately march and to announce to the soldiers that they prepare for a battle tomorrow. How madly we embraced that officer and his Cossacks and immediately let him pass, without letting anyone know. Leaving my picket, I ran to my *druzhina* and announced my joy with indescribable excitement to all listening. Everyone sprang to life. All the rain, hunger and sleeplessness was forgotten for one minute. Everyone congratulated each other and began to hustle about – before the order came from the

General of Cavalry Peter zu Sayn-Wittgenstein. Senior Commander at the Battles of Klyastitsy, 1st and 2nd Polotsk, Chashniki and Smolyani. George Dawe, 1825, oil on canvas, St. Petersburg, State Hermitage Museum.

general to prepare to march, the whole camp came under arms by my word alone. I could have truthfully been punished for it, but at the time everyone forgot such lapses.

Finally we left that hellish place and by nightfall we took to the road. We were ordered not to sing, speak loudly, or make any noise, but we whispered to one another in our excitement and, despite the mud and darkness, travelled 15 *verstas* [16 km] in three hours. The glow of the sky was still visible to us from afar and we grew closer and closer to it. Finally at 9 in the evening, we reached the village of Yurevichi where on the vast plains the corps of General Berg was encamped, constituting the first line of Count Wittgenstein's force. How many times did we stand in camp warming ourselves at our fires without the slightest attention to the image we created? Right before us was a majestic view of a well-dressed corps, the open plain dotted with flickering fires, a magnificent glow wrestling with the dark October night, all manner of artillery and cavalry, rumbling, clattering, voices, movement, life: it all struck us and enveloped our hearts with some new sensation even we ourselves could not describe. We were immediately distributed across the regiments, with whom we then had to fight in the coming battle. The officers of the regular army received us cordially. The sight, the speeches, the greetings, their descriptions of past battles, their jokes and anecdotes – all of it was new for us. We greenhorns met them shyly and awkwardly, answering their questions. However this did not last long as everyone was preparing for battle. The soldiers began to clean their weapons and equipment and we, drying by the fires, curled up on the bare ground where each man stood and slept sweetly. Each of us dreamed of the coming battle, but for many it would be the last dream of their lives.

At dawn on the 6th [18th] of October, we awoke. The sky was overcast but did not rain. With silent reverence everyone formed columns and obeyed every command when given. Our *druzhina* was the last. It was appointed to depart from Yurevichi with the Voronezh [Infantry] Regiment to the forest on the left and to cover 24 guns. As soon as the leading columns left the main road, the shooting began. It was the beginning of a bloody day. The enemy's forward posts, not expecting such a strong attack, were overrun and quickly retreated, firing back as they went. All the while we crossed the field, cavalry troops constantly swept past us, both ours and the enemy's. It was a reconnaissance which our cavalry repelled and we looked at it all with curiosity, not taking part and not even imagining that the battle had begun around us.

Soon we entered the forest. The mud came up to our knees and the terrible path was barely traversable. The horses were unable to pull the guns so naturally we began to drag them. That country road was no more than eight *verstas* [8.53 km] from the field on which the town of Polotsk lay and on which we had to bring our guns, but we had struggled with them in the mud and hillocks for four hours just to bring them to the edge of the woods. All the while, we heard powerful cannonades and our hearts were bursting with impatience. We imagined that the town would be taken without us and that we were too late. In one small grove, we found

Marshal Laurent de Gouvion Saint-Cyr. Commander of the Franco-Bavarian forces defending Polotsk. Henri Rousseau, 1889, engraving, in *Album du Centenaire: Grands Hommes et Grands Faits de la Révolution Française* (Paris: Libraire Furne, Jouvet et Cie, 1889) plate 286.

that the French had only just left their bivouacs and stopped there to rest. We saw their dug-in shelters for the first time, dressed for a long period of military life: frames, doors, and even fireplaces, tables, chairs, couches, and mirrors. It was all gathered by the French from ruined estates in anticipation of spending the winter there. They made a slight error and from the morning of the 6th [12th] of October, they would never see those luxurious homes again.

Around noon, we finally emerged from the woods and turned over our guns, lying down in the bushes to rest. Here for the first time I saw the terrible effect of solid shot. Some unfortunate horse lying nearby had its two forelegs torn off. It was impossible without great pity to look at this poor animal, which almost indifferently lapped the blood from its own wounds. Our rest did not last long. The Voronezh Regiment constituting our first line moved forward but we still remained for a time in the reserve. Noticing our column newly appearing from the woods, the enemy directed several guns entrenched in brick batteries (dismantling a brick factory to build a strong field fortification of sconces and breastworks). Suddenly one cannon ball whizzed over our heads and dug into the earth behind the column. All of us squatted down as if enchanted by a magic wand. What a strange feeling strangled my chest. A feverish shudder ran through my veins. We all looked at each other with distrust and felt privately ashamed of our weakness, and each wanted to encourage his comrades. Then another ball flew over and we flinched the same way. The colonel began to urge us whole-heartily that this bowing was both indecent and useless. I do not remember if we obeyed him through the bombardment, but everyone held a very terrible feeling in his heart nonetheless. All of it was still a game until suddenly one shot fell into the ranks and knocked down two soldiers. That moment was the most painful experience yet we were not given the time however to think about our situation psychologically.

Someone's adjutant galloped up and conveyed an order to the colonel to move forward and reinforce the Voronezh Regiment. This led us against the enemy. That first attempt was very unsuccessful; we did not move far. We had not moved more than a hundred *sazhen*s [213.36 m] when three batteries from only God knows where began to welcome us with solid shot and canister. For five minutes we still advanced with some drunken and numbed perseverance but then all at once and without any source I could know, the whole line could not stand, trembled, and fled backward. We no longer stopped and glanced bewildered at one another as we did at the edge of the forest. That first daring feat did not flatter anyone. The colonel was furious, cursing at us, striking soldiers with his sabre and commanding: 'Stop! Dress!' Somehow we all regained our senses. Shame returned us to our duty. Everyone vied to be the first to encourage his comrades and again the line moved forward smoothly and decisively. Again resumed the shower from the batteries but this time our hearts held firm and the whole *druzhina* pressed forward slowly. Here, to our left, we saw the men of the Voronezh Regiment calmly and orderly retreating and guessed that we would also retreat ahead of them, but did so too quickly. Admitting our first line past us, we noticed at a distance the enemy approaching, stopped and began a firefight. For a quarter of an hour the fire raged on, and for the first time then I heard the music of Charles XII.[26] The whistling of bullets near my ears had already begun to lose its terrible impression on me. Every minute, soldiers and officers dropped out of the line, but many of them fell where they stood. Meanwhile, the enemy approached closer and closer during our fusillade, because our fire, so it seemed, was not terribly lethal for them.

Suddenly the colonel commanded: 'Cease fire! Officers into the line! Charge bayonets! Quick step, march-march! *ura!*' It was finally in our vernacular – finally we were in our own sphere. What a terrible and energizing minute! We quickly strode to meet the enemy and instead of the quick step, we sped up into a full run. The enemy line did not resist, faltered and without waiting for us to arrive,

26   Charles XII reigned as King of Sweden from 1697 to 1718 and was Russia's primary antagonist in the Great Northern War. After several years of small engagements, he elected to deal a decisive blow to Peter the Great's Russia with an invasion in 1708-09 but which concluded with his own defeat at Poltava on 27 June [8 July], 1709. Nearly his entire reign was spent commanding the army and he was said to be more comfortable on the battlefield than anywhere else. His 'music' would be the sound of battle. Ward et al., *Cambridge Modern History*, Vol. 5, pp.584-615.

retreated with all haste, just as we had retreated before. For a moment the colonel stopped us, straightened our formation, and ordered us not to run but instead to march as straight as possible and, without seeing the enemy before us – they having taken cover in the brick entrenchments – he decided to attack. As the joy of our victory washed over us, we forgot about the shot and bullets and our early fears. Talking amongst ourselves, we began to joke and with an amicable shout of 'ura', we marched to the brick sconces, which decently showered us with fire. I remember that beside me there was one glorious sergeant loading his musket as he walked ('just in case', as he said) who was struck by a bullet straight in the forehead between his eyebrows just as he bit open his cartridge and fell backward, still holding the cartridge paper between his lips. And how did I react? At first so recently I was almost moved to tears by the suffering of a dead horse, yet now I laughed at the sight of the cartridge sticking out of his mouth and all the soldiers and officers shared in my amusement. Strange is human nature: how quickly it adapts to fear and suffering that they become easy.

Soon we came to the brick fortifications. We imagined then that there would be a massacre with much bloodshed, but our expectation was not fulfilled. We took the sconces with few losses. Before we reached them, our good artillery, which we had so diligently dragged through the mud, repaid us for our labour. From their first appearance, they turned their fire onto the batteries and fortifications and performed so well that when we reached the slopes, neither gun nor soldier opposed us. The only things in sight were the remnants of that terrible action from our artillery. In fact, it seemed very strange of the enemy to build brick breast-works. They could serve temporary protection against an infantry push but in the first real concentration of artillery, those very bricks shattered and scattered under the twelve-*funt* [4.91 kg] shot, killing the men it was meant to protect. We had seen the proof of it when we entered the abandoned works: piles of enemy bodies lay around the grounds of the former factory; we were very confident that we were innocent in the deaths of all those beneath us. Regardless, we captured the fortifications and were very satisfied and rested there for a quarter of an hour. The colonel, it seems, did not know what to do next, having no further instructions. We calmed down and inspected the battlefield, appearing before us in all its glory.

It was a clear and bright day. Thick clouds of musket smoke were draped majestically over the combatants. Every minute one could hear echoes of the Russian *ura*. Masses of cavalry surged back and forth over the vast plain. To our right was some suburban church that was also turned into a strong fortress and armed on all sides with numerous cannon and to our left was a rather large lake. Behind us was the wide open field and ahead of us was the town of Polotsk, the object of our labours and bloodletting. On the other side of the town was the small River Polota, flowing deep with steep banks, over which there were only two bridges: one on the Sebezh road and the other on the side towards Vitebsk. How long did we admire this magnificent image, not knowing the masses moving around us? Where were they directed and why? Which side was triumphing in the battle? Finally we saw

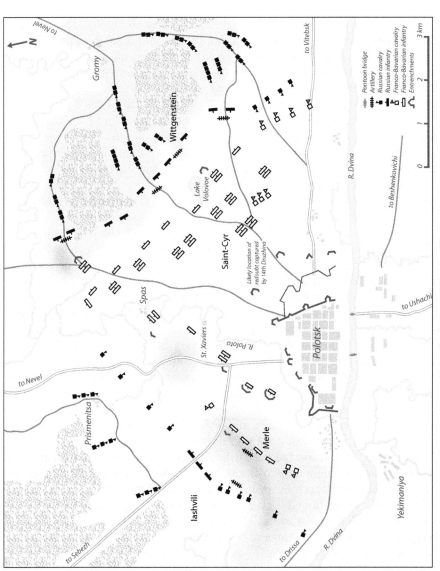

Map of the Second Battle of Polotsk.

our fellows nearby form a column. We emerged from the sconces and saw that it was the 6th *Druzina* heading to experience the enemy's fire for the first time. To their credit it must be said that even though their faces, both the soldiers' and officers', betrayed some confusion and timidity, they courageously marched on and it seemed they did not intend on backing down. But at the moment we forgot that we too were green novices, and saw ourselves as the vanquisher of that Bavarian column which ran from our bayonets, and the conquerors of their brick-works. And because of that, we encouraged our comrades passing by, and even – shamefully – mocked their reluctance. One officer in particular, a German, was very amusing. Moving on the right flank of his platoon, he would try to swat and wave away the bullets whenever they whistled past him and crouched close to the ground with each cannon shot. So recently did we do the same, yet now the sight of it made us laugh!

'What are you doing here?' shouted angrily at us some adjutant, seeing our observational position. 'The Voronezh Regiment again faces a superior enemy and you're standing here with your arms folded!' Our colonel said something in reply and after a short explanation on further actions, he formed us into a closed column and led us to the left where we had already seen a heavy firefight from a distance.[27] We had to cross about half a *versta* [533.4 m] to reach our Voronezh, who wondrously defended against a Bavarian column that previously appeared to be twice their strength and drove at them brazenly. En route, we were greeted with canister from one of the enemy's batteries, such that the colonel had us extend into line again to present smaller targets. We soon united with the Voronezh Regiment and our arrival bolstered their spirits. We joined their right flank and eagerly opened fire. Several times this mutual effort was rather successful, except that while we stood still, the Bavarians continued to move closer and closer to us. Suddenly they stopped firing at us and began to march with levelled bayonets. Their audacity surprised us. The colonel responded in that moment by closing our line and commanded 'charge bayonets', ordering us to firmly strike them back without waiting. There rang out the typical *ura* and our line advanced. The officers departed across the line to their platoons and urged the men to be bold. The Bavarians were not discouraged at all and continued with resolve. A few minutes later, both lines collided and a melee began. Our soldiers were stronger and braver, but inexperienced. In the heat of the fight our line was disordered in various places and twenty Bavarians suddenly broke through our formation. An officer's sword

---

27 When a battalion formed a column of platoons or divisions (pairs of platoons, equal to a company), each subunit stood in a separate line which followed one behind the other. When the column was 'closed', each unit advanced to within three paces of the one ahead. This dense formation could manoeuvre through obstacles easier than a line and was believed to perform well in close combat, but it was vulnerable to artillery fire and brought fewer muskets to bear with its narrow front should it be caught in a firefight. Alexander Zhmodikov and Yuriy Zhmodikov, *Tactics of the Russian Army in the Napoleonic Wars* (West Chester, Ohio: Nafziger Collection, 2003), Vol. 1, pp11-13.; *Military Regulations of 1811*, p.184.

was no equal weapon against their bayonets. One officer named Leontyev was the first victim of this inequity: several bayonets to the chest collapsed him to the ground unconscious. (He would later recover and said that having a cold bayonet plunge into his chest was the most horrible feeling.) Our lieutenant colonel, the venerable sexagenarian who had been wounded beforehand by a canister ball but remained in the line regardless, was knocked down by a blow to the head with a musket butt. He fell to the ground, cursed at his Bavarian with strong Russian words and while lying on the ground still knocking away their bayonets with his sword. All of this transpired in no more than two minutes. The penetrating Bavarians were all stabbed, the line was closed up as much as possible, and in two minutes the whole Bavarian column was overthrown. Without hearing a command, our bearded heroes[28] chased after them from behind, stabbing them as they ran. A great effort and even flogging was needed from the colonel to halt and reassemble those brave men, even more so truly at the moment when the commander of the *corps de bataille*[29] sent the cavalry (the Yamburg Dragoons) to complete the defeat of the Bavarian column.

Halting again in an inactive position, the colonel waited for instructions and when he received them, we formed a closed column and marched with the Voronezh Regiment to the reserve, and both of our units only deployed a platoon each of sharpshooters to observe the enemy. Volunteers were requested and from our *druzhina* came both I and my comrade Groten. We gathered around 90 sharpshooters and after crossing ourselves, we went forward and spread out into a chain. On the wide open field, where the battle had covered ten *verstas* [10.67 km], we could not see anyone. The battle was raging to our right and we, approaching a chain of enemy sharpshooters, began to exchange fire with them very amicably without doing much damage. My comrade accompanied me the whole way. He was the son of a wealthy merchant and conversed with me in our spare time, asking me to take his wallet and gold watch if he were killed. No sooner had he uttered this request than a bullet struck him in the forehead and he fell beside me. I looked over him bitterly, shook my head and sent two soldiers to carry him back to our column, forgetting his wishes. This occurrence greatly surprised and upset me. I ran to all my shooters and told them that we should repay the enemy for the death of our comrade. They obeyed me and we rushed forward furiously at those

---

28   Unlike in the regular army, peasants levied by the militia were not forcibly shaved. *Complete Collection of Laws*, Collection 1, Vol. 29, p.923. No. 22,390.

29   The centre of the army, as opposed to the left and right wings or the reserve. Wittgenstein's centre was commanded by Lieutenant General Gregor von Berg (Grigoriy Maksimovich Berg). The 14th *Druzhina* however was initially placed in the reserve of the left column, which had its own *corps de bataille* under Major General Ivan Matveyevich Begichev. Модест Богданович, *История Отечественной Войны 1812 года* (St. Petersburg: Торговый дом Струговщика, Похитонова, Водова и Ко., 1860), Vol. 3, p.450. [Modest Bogdanovich, *History of the Patriotic War of 1812* (St. Petersburg: Firm of Strugovshchik, Pokhitonov, Vodov and Co., 1860), Vol. 3, p.450.]

handfuls of the enemy skirmishers fleeing. Breaking through their chain naturally, we ran upon some battery from which we never heard a shot but in front of which was a ditch and palisades, so we consulted with an old NCO from the army on what to do.

'We are too few, Your Nobleness. We'll die here for nothing. Falling back some to our column would be best'. I heeded his advance then and quickly pulled the men back along the same path we had come. From a distance we saw a huge black mass of enemy cavalry rushing toward our direction. We immediately turned to the right and managed to run to the empty brick sconces which we previously captured. In that place, our rear was secured but instead of hiding in the hole and lurking, we clung together in a mass and waited for whatever would happen. In two minutes the cavalry we saw from afar was now before us. They were French cuirassiers. The sun glinted off their armour, the horsetails of their helmets waved in the air, the earth trembled under the stamping hooves of their horses – in short, they made a magnificent sight. I paid dearly for this spectacle. That whole enormous mass swept past us to some unknown destination without paying us any attention except for the occasional look of contempt. But it seemed indecent to watch the enemy without trying to shoot at him, so I ordered my force and they eagerly began their work. These sudden shots astonished the riders and struck them in the flank, knocking several men out of the saddle. They continued on their route however, threatening us with their broadswords, and we continued to answer with bullets, inwardly rejoicing that we had managed to kill around 50 enemies who could not do anything about it because of their own objective. The whole column had almost ridden by when suddenly we saw with some concern that the rear squadrons stopped and turned around to face us and began to encircle our mass. We continued shooting. Cursing us without mercy, they closed in more and more around us. In several minutes I noticed that our fire had died down.

'Why aren't you shooting together, boys?'

'Well, sir, Your Nobleness, we've run out of cartridges', they answered, and it was then that I realized our situation was very dire. The cuirassiers finally surrounded us and their commander shouted at us that we should surrender. I translated it for my soldiers but most replied: 'We won't put our lives in the hands of infidels.[30] Perhaps God will help and ours will come to the rescue'. I shouted back our refusal and the last of our cartridges were spent hastily. Then the cuirassiers plunged into us and the massacre began. Each man could not think about saving himself,

---

30 In the common vernacular, foreign nationals and foreign faiths were nearly interchangeable, and 'басурман, infidel', appears in the mouths of peasants and militiamen in propaganda from 1812-1814, as, for example, *Руской Ратник Иван Гвоздила, и Руской Милицийской Мужик Долбила*, ca. 1812, woodcut. Reproduced in Gulevich, *History of the Leib-Guard Finland Regiment*, unnumbered plate between pp.24-25. [*Russian Warrior Ivan Gvozdila and Russian Militiaman-Peasant Dolbila*, ca. 1812, woodcut. Reproduced in Gulevich, *History of the Leib-Guard Finland Regiment*, unnumbered plate between pp.24-25].

only making his life as costly as possible to take and each man fell very satisfied, so long as he succeeded first in stabbing one of the cuirassiers with his bayonet. This entertainment lasted for about half an hour, I believe, and every moment my cluster of men dwindled until I was alone, leaning back against the bricks. Several times an enemy officer cried out to me that I should surrender, but I answered him with curses. Finally they reached me. Their work did not take long. I did not fall from the first two blows to the head of their broadswords and harmlessly defended myself with my smallsword [or spadroon], and I remember wounding one on the thigh and jabbing another in the ribs; I do not remember which one of them awarded me with a pistol shot for it. Then another casually hit me in the neck and another in the foot. I collapsed and was showered with blows and curses like a torrent. I was wearing my frock, tailcoat, and a padded jacket, and the backpack over the top of all that, all of which was chopped into coleslaw, yet only the two blows to the head felt threatening. One in my hand was insignificant but another seriously jabbed me in the back with his broadsword from the saddle. All the other strikes failed to pierce my clothing. Believing me to be hacked to ribbons, they left me alone at last. When I heard them leave, I opened my eyes.

Streams of blood flowed from my head and pleasantly warmed my skin. The instinct of self-preservation however inspired me to try to stop the bleeding. Gathering all of my strength, I untied my sash (which was knitted, no less[31]) and bound it tightly around my head and stretched myself out over the bricks, surrendering myself to the Almighty. Either from the loss of blood or the fatigue of the whole day, I felt compelled to sleep. I do not know how long I slept, but a doctor told me after that I would have many nights ahead of me if our *druzhina* had not returned to that place. The unit suffered badly as well from that cavalry charge and the cuirassiers were diabolical. From the left, the Voronezh Regiment and two *druzhina*s withstood their very heavy fire; from the right, twelve guns showered them with canister; and from the rear the Yamburg Dragoons wheeled around them. In this scenario, the whole mass of cavalry, leaving half of its men in place, rushed back as quickly as they had rushed forward. The Yamburg Dragoons gave chase and behind them followed the infantry columns.

They reached the brick sconces, our *druzhina* discovered our massacre, recognized their own and carried me off when they saw I was still alive. When I awoke, three men were carrying me. I asked them to stop but I do not know why. They indulged me and I asked them simply: 'where are you taking me?'

'To bandage your wounds'. And then I remembered and felt everything that happened. How stupid I feel now about that minute of pause, as it cost the life of

---

31   Russian officers' sashes were meant to be silver metal thread alternated with stripes of orange and black silk, but in 1812, cheaper alternatives made of affordable fibres were permitted for officers with financial woes. Viskovatov, *Historical Description of Dress and Armament*, Vol. 10, p.342.

one of my rescuers. As soon as they lifted me up again and carried me, suddenly with great pain I felt a soldier behind let go of me with a violent jerk.

'What the hell are you doing, bastard?' I said with a groan. But he did not answer. A cannon ball struck him diagonally and nearly tore him in half. I shuddered and asked the other two to somehow get me on my feet and lead me away as quickly as possible. Limping with as much strength as I still had, I dragged myself to the place where the wounded were being treated. Dear God! What a horrible sight! That place was much worse than the carnage of the battlefield. The doctors, soaked in blood, rushed like maniacs from one to another and barely had time to give aid. Soon one of those Asclepiuses came to me and asked where I was wounded.[32] 'Everywhere!' I replied, and he looked me over, shook his head and did not know where to start. Seeing my hacked clothes, he figured that each cut was a wound and assumed, I believe, that it was useless to bandage me. Regardless, he started with my head. Untying the sash, he wanted to remove my forage cap but the blood had clotted and it stuck to me. I asked him to cut it off so that removing it would not hurt much. He however disagreed, and as much as the general haste of the day allowed him, he ripped the hat off and looked quite calmly at the wound beneath, threw two *funt* [819.03 g] of old linens on me, wrapped me in bandages and then moved on to the rest of my body. 'What? Are my wounds fatal?' I asked with my heart pounding in my chest.

'It's impossible to know right now', he said indifferently. 'The first dressing will decide everything – pray to God. It seems however that only one blow to the head damaged the skull and then not badly. Perhaps God will intercede'. He said all of this over my painful moaning, extracted from me by the barbers removing a boot from my wounded foot. The bullet came down with surprising luck straight into the flesh and, without breaking out of the boot, remained in the sole. The doctor took it and told me that to be safe he had to cut off that part of the foot and that he was then going to run and fetch his instruments with which one of his fellows was performing at the moment.

A cold sweat ran over me. I was terribly frightened of being cut up, even for a small part of my foot, but how do you argue with the autocracy of a doctor? He left and something held him up. At that time another passed by me and asked whether my wound had been examined. With a sorry voice, I stopped him and begged him to see my foot and determine if it needed to be cut. He leaned over, stuck his fingers into the wound (and I kept silent!) and he declared that the bone was undamaged and that there was not the slightest cause for amputation. I joyfully grasped him and did not let him go until the first doctor returned. Then they began to argue with each other in German, but as God revealed that tongue to me, I entered the conversation and with the sweetest courtesy urged

---

32 Asclepius was the Greek god of medicine and patron of physicians. Andreyevskiy et al., *Brockhaus and Efron Dictionary*, s.v. 'Эскулап.' [Andreyevskiy et al., *Brockhaus and Efron Dictionary*, s.v. 'Asclepius.']

them not to touch my feet. With displeasure the second doctor yielded to the first, saying that he wanted to do it for my sake and asked where else I was wounded. 'Nowhere else! That's all! I'm fine!' I shouted, keeping silent about the other cuts because I was afraid of his willingness to operate. After bandaging the leg, they left me and after I waited for half an hour, I lay down against a log and fell asleep.

When I woke up again, it was dusk. Numerous fires were burning on the plains, the shooting had stopped, the Grodno Hussars bustled around us, and by the disposition of our forces we intended to spend the night there. The first thing I asked was if we had taken Polotsk, and the reply was 'no!' This news upset me very much. So many had died for that, I thought, yet the goal of the battle was not yet achieved. 'Have we been broken?' I asked.

'Oh no!' the hussars told me. 'The French were driven into the town and tomorrow, truly, we'll go on the attack. As a matter of fact, they camped here all summer and threatened to march on Peter's. After today's trouble, they'll be running home quickly'.

Thanking the hussar for the news, I began to watch their activities with great interest. They were cooking buckwheat porridge and gathering to eat. I remember being on a very strict diet for two days, and in my hunger I imagined the hussars' slop as the finest delicacy. 'What are you preparing there?' I asked in the most diplomatic tone.

'The usual, Your Nobleness, porridge! If you don't want to try some, we won't hold it against you'.

'Nonsense, brother, give me a taste'. I dragged myself to the fire over which hung the communal cauldron, armed myself with a wooden spoon and sat down to the meal. 'What's that white thing sticking out of the pot, brother?' I asked.

'That, sir, is a tallow candle... for flavour'. The candle dampened my enthusiasm and I wondered whether I should eat the porridge or not. Eventually hunger won the debate. I sipped a spoonful, then another, then a third, and did not stop until I was full. I gave my thanks to the hussars and offered them twenty kopecks but they were offended and refused to accept it.

My wounds won me universal respect. Everywhere I went, people troubled over me and I was put up in a warmer and softer quarters (the night being very cold). By their generosity, I slept soundly until morning.

In the morning, several wagons arrived to carry the wounded back to Yurevichi and I took the moment to inquire about my fellows. Of the 16 officers, only two remained unscathed: the colonel and his adjutant. Out of the 800 men in the *druzhina*, 96 men could still stand in the line.

Somehow we hobbled our way to Yurevichi by noon and all the wounded men of our *druzhina* were crammed into one hut. At that point, our baggage train caught up with us and our diet ended. By evening, we heard heavy gunfire again, saw the glow of the town in the distance and could not retire to bed until a Cossack brought us news that Polotsk had been taken!

II

On the night of the 7th and 8th [19th and 20th] of October, we did not sleep for almost the whole night. The joyous news of the capture of Polotsk and the captivating sight of the distant fire produced an impotent anger at the retreating enemy – it incensed all of our hearts. We were also troubled by envy. The city had been taken, the enemy was put to flight, but we were not involved in these exploits. We had only moistened the fields of Polotsk with our blood. Shameful! In the morning, the glow of the fire in the sky died out and fell asleep. The next day, we received orders to relocate the wounded to the town. Many refused to make the journey due to their painful wounds and remained in Yurevichi. I, along with most of my fellow-sufferers, was burning with impatience to reach the promised Polotsk, newly conquered. We sat four to a cart and the modest horse lashed to it pulled us along the main road with a rather cheerful spirit. The large cobbles, which occasionally paved that Belarussian highway, had a very unpleasant effect on our ride. We continually yelled and groaned, yet never stopped our heated arguments about the martial and political subjects of the day.

Soon the most unparalleled spectacle unfurled before us. The whole field from the battle of the 6th [18th] of October lay before us, still fresh and littered with piles of bodies, disabled gun carriages, crates, empty batteries and dying horses. The autumn grass was blackened in places by dried blood. Everywhere reigned a gloomy silence, sorrow and destruction. There, where for two days 400 guns thundered, where the air was split by incessant cheers of 'ura', where the ground shook with the trampling of thousands of horses, now a sad silence was draped over all that space and over all the remnants of a terrible battle like a veil of death and oblivion. Only the slow creaking of the wagon wheels and the voices of four dismal casualties broke that silence. On the left of the road I could see the dilapidated church which harried us so strongly with its cannon on the 6th. Further on the horizon was the lake which covered our left flank, but I strained with all my might in vain to spot the memorable brick fortifications which were nowhere to be seen. It seemed to even wound my pride. That place where I so bravely risked my head beneath the swords of their cuirassiers, where I collapsed under their blows – that place was razed to the ground. The poor fate of all human affairs! Their care, labour, everything they sacrificed, if should it shine, and then what? With a little time, not only are they and their works forgotten, but even the best monuments of their actions vanish from the face of the earth.

Riding into the town over the hastily repaired bridge, we recalled with proud self-satisfaction that the first force to breech the walls of Polotsk were the militia (the 12th *Druzhina* specifically). At the gates, we found and hired a guide to take us to our quarters. At this end of the town it was so peaceful and quiet but in the distance, at the other end, shots could be heard every minute. There on the Dvina, our militia was labouring under enemy bullets and cannonballs. The French naturally burned down the bridge during their retreat and now we were hurrying to build another. The enemy batteries, placed along the edge of the forest on the opposite bank, prevented us in a very unpleasant manner, but our soldiers became accustomed to the accompaniment and merely cursed whenever the shots interrupted them.

Our hospital-quarters were placed in the home of some Jew or other, and fourteen wounded officers of field- and company-grade were put up in one room, which only had a single bed and a few wooden chairs.[33] But we were in Polotsk and the thought lent charm to every nook and cranny. Here we were dining under proper roofs for the first time since our day in Nevel. We had soup with tenderized beef – what a luxury! Our colonel's adjutant came to us and told us news which further heightened our happy position. Wittgeinstein had received an envelope from the Sovereign with the written instruction: 'open upon the capture of Polotsk' – and it was already captured. The letter was a decree promoting him to the rank of full general. We naturally drank a toast to the newly promoted general's health and our high spirits were all the higher. The whole night was filled with friendly conversation and cheer. That evening, we bought hay, straw and a few dirty mattresses, while the one real bed was given up to the most senior officer, our 60-year-old lieutenant colonel. He was wounded when the Bavarians broke through our line during the melee. But the good veteran did not want any advantage and descended to the floor on the soft straw. He told the room that he thought it should be given to me! What a triumph for my pride! I pleaded on the side of modesty but to no avail, the room agreed with his decision and the bed was mine for being the most thoroughly covered in wounds. I never before had such pleasant dreams or such proud satisfaction.

The next morning was the most unpleasant for everyone. It was the first day of dressing all of the wounded and the condition of their dressings would decide their fate. If a wound had festered, then it was likely it could be cured, but if the wound did not create any discharge but was still found to be inflamed, then the victim should write his will.[34] The agony I suffered during this procedure surpasses all description. Long and thick hairs, lint and clotted blood made such a dense mass that the doctor could not proceed. He told me I needed to be shaved. The barber immediately went to work and everything went well until he reached the wounds, where it was necessary for the razor to touch the offending sites and the pain was

---

33   Junior or company officers encompass the ranks of ensign to captain (grades XIV-XI) and senior or field officers encompass major to colonel (grades VIII-VI). In Russian these terms are taken from the German 'Oberoffizier' and 'Stabsoffizier' respectively. Shepelyov, *Titles, Uniforms and Orders*, pp.117-118.

34   Pus indicates that the immune system is fighting infection, while inflammation without pus can indicate that the wound is still infected but the immune system is failing. The belief that pus was necessary to proper healing can be traced back to Hippocrates and well predates germ theory. M. M. Manring, Alan Hawk, Jason Calhoun and Romney Andersen, 'Treatment of Wounds: A Historical Review,' *The National Center for Biotechnology Information*, last modified 2009. https://www.ncbi.nlm.nih.gov/pmc/articles/PMC2706344/

unbearable. Anguished sweat ran down my face in large drops. No matter how ashamed I was to shout in that room full of my fellows, I could not stand the torment and was constantly yelling and cursing. At last the terrible operation ended and the doctor washed himself again to examine the wounds. He told me that they did not seem dangerous. I felt for a while that that was the case, but I will confess that the doctor's confirmation was an extreme relief. I then began to strongly consider myself to be among the living again and immediately started writing letters to my mother and friends, telling them about my exploits with pompous modesty.

On the same day, all the wounded were transferred to the Jesuit College. It was one of the most famous institutions of that famous brotherhood in all of Europe.[35] It housed 6,000 souls from the province of Vitebsk and in order to keep them safe from the greed of the French, they paid them a levy of a million francs and four months of provisions for the whole headquarters of the Marshals Oudinot and Saint-Cyr. They took us in with warmth and care. More than 300 officers were placed in the cells and along the hallways of that huge building and the excellent table put out demonstrated the art of their chefs and the culinary gifts of those Brothers in Christ. The Sovereign Emperor granted a ruble's worth of provisions per day to the wounded officers and we naturally donated this sum to our hosts but with a noble selflessness they refused to be paid and fed us for a whole month gratis, letting us keep the allocated funds as pocket money. Moreover, twice a day a Jesuit would come around and ask if we needed anything.

I had the opportunity to meet two of them somewhat briefly. One was a 60-year-old Italian and the other – imagine my initial surprise! – was a Russian noble and landowner from Kostroma. He was educated by the brotherhood as a youth, fell in love with their spirit and decided to join them when he came of age. At first appearance, we found it distasteful, but little by little we came to terms with it and even developed a friendship with that semi-apostate due to his continual, helpful, and pleasant care for us. Both of my new acquaintances gave me a multitude of rare and curious books on my request and I spend my time of secluded convalescence productively, taking lessons in Greek and Polish from them. When my wounds were well enough that I could leave the cloister, the better community of officers had assembled at the commandant's and the *Platz*-major's.[36] Both were from the militia. The 12th *Druzhina* was the first to break into Polotsk and so their

---

35   After the Papal Bull suppressing the Society of Jesus (the Jesuits) in 1773, the order was expelled from Polish-Lithuania but lived on in the Russian territories annexed from the Commonwealth, and Polotsk's academy became a primary centre for the order, especially on 12 [24] January, 1812, when it was elevated above all other Jesuit schools in the Russian Empire by Imperial decree. Andreyevskiy et al., *Brockhaus and Efron Dictionary*, s.v. 'Иезуиты.' [Andreyevskiy et al., *Brockhaus and Efron Dictionary*, s.v. 'Jesuits.']

36   The 'Place-major' was second to the commandant in command of a city or fortress's contingent and oversaw prisoners, assignment of new recruits, and guard mountings. *Complete Collection of Laws*, Collection 1, Vol. 43, Part 1 (1796-1800), p.13. No. 17,805.

Colonel Nikolev was made commandant and their Major Galchyonkov the *Platz*-major in the newly liberated town. The latter in particular was distinguished by his true Russian hospitality and generous courtesy.

We soon received wondrous news. Moscow had been freed and Napoleon was retreating! The battles at Tarutino and Maloyaroslavets, attaining for us the most exaggerated forms, assured us that the French Army was completely broken and that we only needed to clobber them as they ran. We remembered our feelings and our conversations on that field of epiphany where we first learned of the loss of Moscow. Such depression, such a gloomy hopelessness had captured our hearts then. But now all of the sudden the war made an unexpected reversal! All of armed Europe, led by the premier commander and invading Russia with such certain expectation of imminent profit, were now fleeing and abandoning all their cannons, wagons and thousands of men to become prisoners. Our joy was impossible to describe. It needed to be felt personally and in the moment, holy and without equal! We were all rushing about like madmen, laughing, embracing each other, and only occasionally regretting that our older brothers in the main army, in their victory, left us so little work. Is it any wonder that in such a frame of mind, we recovered from our wounds like the *bogatyr*s of legend?[37]

The power of a young and healthy constitution soon began to heal my wounds in the fastest manner. In less than a month, I was able to walk everywhere and with that, my first and incessant desire was to return to the army as soon as possible. Everyone dissuaded me, scolded me or even wanted to have me sent to Pskov (where my mother lived), but I scolded them in turn and refused to obey. My head wounds were healed, and others were of no consequence. What else was there to consider? I wanted to surprise everyone and return to the army a month later with my wounds half healed, but one small thing delayed me for another week. Definitely determined to go, I went to the baths two days before my journey as according to Russian tradition, and since I had not been in three months, I bolted for the sauna with a strong sense of Russian bravado. Suddenly one of my comrades with a terrified expression told me that blood was flowing down my face. My head of course was bound up and doused with cold water, but despite that, one wound had opened and the blood, seeping through the bandages, flowed down my cheeks. All the heat of my bathhouse poetry immediately turned cold, like the icy cowardice of animalistic self-preservation, and my recent boasting became the most humble temperance. I hurried home quickly but the whole matter resolved itself almost by fear alone. The doctor scolded me for going to the bath without consulting him first, bandaged my head and for a week I again demanded my

---

37   A 'богатыр' (*bogatyr*) was a stock heroic character of great vitality, martial ability, religious devotion, and sometimes patriotism that appeared in oral epic poems and folk songs, the first large printed collection of which was published in 1804. Andreyevskiy et al., *Brockhaus and Efron Dictionary*, s.v. 'Богатыри.'; *Ibid.*, s.v. 'Былины.' [Andreyevskiy et al., *Brockhaus and Efron Dictionary*, s.v. 'Bogatyri.'; *Ibid.*, s.v. 'Byliny.']

release back to the army. No one needed to keep me, so at last I took to flight down the beautiful winter roads to return to my *druzhina*.

In 1812, the transition from autumn to winter was remarkably fast. On the 10th [22nd] of October, we still looked out from our cell through the open window and enjoyed the warm, beautiful evening on the picturesque banks of the Dvina, crowned with batteries and terminating in the very prosaic forests and swamps. By the 18th [30th], the Dvina was already frozen, the fields were covered with snow and the Russian winter had enlisted in the auxiliaries of our army.

With such joy I flew to catch up with our corps as quickly as possible! With such delight I looked on the fields of Chashniki and Smolyani where Wittgenstein defeated his third French marshal (Victor), who opposed him.[38] The snow concealed half the bloody traces of the local battles, but what remained in sight was all the more striking and picturesque. Here the militia had many experiences of bravery, but was more sensible in its actions and better led.

The closer I rode to our corps, the more important became the news. The Cossacks told me that Napoleon himself, it seemed, would fall into the hands of Wittgenstein. I lost my breath while trying to catch up to such a famous confrontation. By the 15th [27th] of November, I reached the camp for our detachment. What cheery news awaited me there? The immortal days at Krasnyy, which gave Kutuzov the name of Smolenskiy,[39] rang through all the rumours. Napoleon's army was said to be shattered to pieces, all its guns were seized, and the remains of those ravaged regiments were harried to the Berezina River where they awaited the final defeat. The weather helped the Russian arms completely. The early winter proved to be unreliable and a thaw set in, a circumstance which all said would terribly ruin Napoleon as the Berezina would break and flow again. Napoleon certainly had to cross it to retreat. In view of Chichagov's[40] army waiting for him

---

38 Claude Victor-Perrin, Duke de Belluno was defeated at Smolyani on 1-2 [13-14] November, 1812. Steinheil, *Notes Regarding the St. Petersburg Militia*, Vol. 1, pp.164-167.

39 Field Marshal Mikhail Illarionovich Golenishchev-Kutuzov was awarded the title 'Serene Prince of Smolensk' for his victory at Krasnyy or Krasnoy, since the nearby city of Smolensk was liberated as a direct result and Krasnyy itself was too obscure a village for a victory title. The battle was the first instance in 1812 of Napoleon personally losing the field, but the tactical victory failed to effect serious or lasting damage to the Grand Armée. This victory title expanded his surname to Golenishchev-Kutuzov-Smolenskiy but he frequently signed his name as only 'Prince K.-Smolenskiy' in his letters and reports thereafter. Ward et al., *Cambridge Modern History*, Vol. 9, pp.500-501.; Beskrovnyy ed., *M. I. Kutuzov: Collection of Documents*, Vol. 4, Part 2, pp.545-558.

40 Admiral Pavel Vasilyevich Chichagov assumed command of the Danubian Army after Kutuzov moved to St. Petersburg and marched it north to combine with the Reserve Observational Army, drive the Austrian corps out of Belarus, and then try to cut off Napoleon's retreat from the west. He would fail in trapping the Grand Armée, suffering public disgrace for it, and ultimately resign his post on 2 [13] February, 1813. Bogdanovich, *History of the Patriotic War of 1812*, Vol. 3, pp.205-295.; Модест Богданович, *История Войны 1813 года за Независимость Германии* (St. Petersburg: Типография Штаба Военно-Учебных Заведений, 1863), Vol. 1, pp.11-12. [Modest Bogdanovich, *History of the War of 1813 for the*

on the other side, he had to construct new bridges. The crossing of the river had to be done all the while fighting with Wittgenstein, who waited for him on the right bank, and escaping the onslaught of Platov, whose sabres whistled in his ears.

When I came to the colonel, no one could believe my speedy recovery. When they saw my bandages, not removed yet as a precaution and for their warmth, they all scolded me and said that my early arrival was either boasting or stupidity. I did not make excuses because I was not conscious of the real reason for my haste. Only now do I understand it: it was simply youth and nothing more.

Our *druzhina*, greatly diminished even with the return of the wounded from the hospitals (200 men out of 800), was placed in the rearguard. I was somewhat encumbered in my attire but the colonel allowed me to keep it as it was when I arrived: I did not have a warm greatcoat, because I gave away the one I received in St. Petersburg to our battalion adjutant after the Battle of Polotsk, as he was wounded in the abdomen by a bullet – that poor man did now follow us from Yurevichi to Polotsk and after several days he died; instead the company commander gave me his skeepskin coat padded with cotton, and from the same man I was girded with a sabre, since I inadvertently left my original sword at the brick fortifications which witnessed my brave exploits. On my head I wore a fur cap with earflaps but one of my feet was left unprotected against the cold and warmed itself only by walking day and night and remaining close to the fire.

Nonetheless, my most fervent wish came true: I was back in the army! What a powerful moment! The bloody drama of the invasion was reaching its climax, apparently, and I was one of its actors; although truthfully I was an extra, I still stood on the stage. This revelry was such fodder for the imagination of a 17-year-old officer! What scenarios in which to excel and be glorified would present themselves? But alas, could anyone be so deceived in their hopes and expectations?

For the whole of the 15th [27th] of November, a powerful cannonade thundered around us and our rearguard attentively stood still in place. We bit our lips and chewed our nails impatiently to no avail, and we fruitlessly stopped each Cossack that passed by– no one had even a passing thought about us. Could anything be more offensive? Come nightfall however, we learned through prisoners that Napoleon would only appear tomorrow. On that night, Partouneaux's whole division surrendered when surrounded by our forces. A new height! Even in that feat we did not participate. However, on the 16th [28th] of November, we hoped to be indulged and were rewarded completely.

With the break of dawn, gunfire rattled again from all sides and we were ordered to advance. Imagine our joy! So many scenes like we saw at Polotsk did we expect that day! Napoleon himself was our opponent! Such glory, such an opportunity for greatness! But fate decided to be cruel to us on that day. The famous crossing,

Independence of Germany (St. Petersburg: Press of the Staff of Military Educational Institutions, 1863), Vol. 1, pp.11-12.]

which will be remembered for a thousand years, which has been described by so many both historically and romantically, and which will provide future legions of writers with such abundant material for striking portraits, touching scenes and philosophical discourses, took place two *verstas* [2.13 km] away from us sinners, who stood on a height and covered the 12-gun battery of General Fock[41], seeing only from a distance the shapeless, undulating masses of the enemy that crowded around the river and pushed one another over the bridges. Before this mass stood several columns of French who repelled all of our efforts to close in on the crossing with surprising courage. Finally, either from our shots or from the weight of the people shuffling on the bridges, one of the spans collapsed and the crossing came to an end. I describe the crossing, but there it was before me, an image of horrors, weeping, and despair. The French Army had almost completely crossed the river already in those two days, but the baggage and all the non-combatants remained on our side. They all crowded, huddled, fought their way to the river and to the bridge but it was not there, and the advance of the crowd, squeezed by the masses behind, were cast into the river where they struggled against the waves and tried to swim across, grabbing onto ice flows and screaming and dying with desperate cries. It is impossible to convey or describe these sights. They belong only to the most frenzied and monstrous poetry. The historian or novelist cannot describe to you in some weak essay that fearsome crossing and that fact alone will make every writer tremble. From two *verstas* away from the bridge on the height we could see and understand every evil taking place, but the terrifying cries of despair from all the masses of dying people were heard so clearly and our hearts were so strongly shocked by it that we stupidly asked more than once of our colonel to try to save them from the disaster. We forgot that enemy columns stood between them and us.

Everything was quiet by evening. Our corps completely retired to bivouac, lit fires and then broke into arguments, debates, and speculations. What did it all mean? How was Napoleon allowed to cross? How was he allowed to build his bridges? Why did Chichagov's force not trample him back into the water when he came across to the western side? How did Kutuzov not follow on his heels to the river and deliver the final blow? All of these questions took up nearly our whole night. Naturally all of us, as significant and well-informed individuals, primarily condemned Chichagov, then Kutuzov, and finally even our Wittgenstein. The whole Battle of Berezina appeared to us as a weak, sluggish and degraded act.

---

41 Major General Aleksandr Borisovich Fock or Foch (Fok) was Chief of Staff of the Corps of Finland at the outbreak of the 1812 campaign and commanded Wittgenstein's reserve during the Battle of the Berezina. Виктор Безотосный (ed.), *Энциклопедия 'Отечественная Война 1812 года'*, (Moscow: Российская Политическая Энциклопедия, 2004), s.v. 'Финляндский Корпус'.; Ibid., s.v. 'Березинская Переправа'. [Viktor Bezotosnyy (ed.), *The 'Patriotic War of 1812' Encyclopedia*, (Moscow: Russian Political Encyclopedia, 2004), s.v. 'Finland Corps'.; Ibid., s.v. 'The Crossing of the Berezina'.]

January Suchodolski, Crossing the Berezina. 1866, oil on canvas, National Museum in Poznan.

'Deliver us, God, from such judges!'[42]

The next morning opened again with a cannonade. But this was a solemn festival, a final farewell to the French Army, courtesy of the Russian nation. We could still see there the remnants of that great army, struggling greatly, resisting valiantly and it could be said that the genius of Napoleon and the spirit of his warriors still flashed there. Beyond the Berezina all of that disappeared. After half an hour of our artillery salute, the French set fire to the remaining bridge and all gunnery ceased. This meant that the rest had made it across. We became quite the hosts then on the right bank and hurried to the place of yesterday's battle and the terrible crossing. There we found the grave images become even more striking, as

42 A quotation from Ivan Krylov's telling of the fable 'The Ass and the Nightingale', in which an igno-rant donkey critiques the artful singing of a nightingale with a comparison to a rooster and the insult drives the talented bird from the forest. Zotov means to say that he and his fellow officers were not experienced or well-enough informed to assess the decisions and performance of the army's leadership. Демьян Бедный (ed.), *Полное Собрание Сочинений Ивана Крылова* (Moscow: Государственное Издательство Художественной Литературы, 1946), Vol.3, pp.55-56. [Demyan Bednyy (ed.), *The Complete Collection of Works by Ivan Krylov* (Moscow: State Publishing House of Fictional Literature, 1946), Vol.3, pp.55-56].

the dying were not in a single mass but were spread all over in varying groups. For a whole *versta* [1.07 km] it was impossible to reach the bank for the remains of the French train. Carriages, carts, wagons, foppish barouches, droshkies – everything was loaded up with Russian goods stolen in Moscow and from all the towns along the way; smashed guns, powder crates, thousands of packhorses quietly looking for food in the snow or in the various wagons; finally, on the piles of the dead and dying were crowds of women and children, hungry and half-frozen. All of it cluttered the way such that a whole *druzhina* of the militia was detached to clear a path to the crossing. There the sight was even worse. The whole river was full of the dead. In revolting groups emerging from the water were those who died the day before and along the shore, like phantoms of the River Styx, roamed crowds of others who looked across the river at our arrival numbly and without any worry or response to our questions. Both the officers and soldiers brought these unfortunates with them in order to feed them, wrap them with anything warmer and then send them to Vitebsk. For all of our original anger at the French, the disaster on the Berezina seemed enough to us to come to terms with them for the fires and the destruction of our towns and villages, for the countless murders of the residents therein, and for the thousands lost in battle. We did not imagine then that the horrors on the Berezina were just the beginning of a perilous period and that the invasion was only an entry in that calamitous chapter of history. Beyond the Berezina awaited them death and destruction a hundred times more terrible.

When tabulating and clearing away the baggage many of us enriched ourselves, some inadvertently, other deliberately. Several officers collected books, paintings, and atlases. The devout sought out ecclesiastical vestments and utensils. More practical people loved money, flatware, spoons, bowls, samovars, and so on. The lazy received nothing, and I, shamefully, belonged to that latter group! For two whole days we continued to investigate and remove the wreckage and more than half was left where it lay.

The bridges across the Berezina were repaired in those two days and we began to march in pursuit of the French, which relieved Chichagov's army, who were completely exhausted and consigned to let Napoleon escape, being still much weaker than him. On the 20th of November [2nd of December], we converged with Chichagov's force and, letting them pass ahead, gave them all the laurels to be won for harrying the enemy. From that moment began the terrible period of the French retreat. The thaw, hindering Napoleon's crossing so much over the Berezina, suddenly turned into such severe frosts which even we in St. Petersburg had rarely seen before. The cold intensified daily and continually stopped between -23° and -25° Réaumur [-28.75° and 31.25° Celsius]. It was already the last, insurmountable blow for the French Army. Its moral condition was completely collapsed. Each camp, each night, was as terrible as a lost battle; thousands died in the greatest agony. The soldiers, each a possible survivor of Austerlitz, Eylau, and Borodino, now fell into our hands very cheaply. Each Cossack took tens of them prisoner at a time and led them in a nearly unconscious condition. They knew nothing, remembered nothing, and understood nothing. The roads were strewn with their corpses, and their stragglers were scattered throughout all the huts and cabins without charity.

During the march from Kosina to Dolginovo, I inadvertently saved a Swiss captain. We passed by a forest and the snow was hard and shallow. Because we were enjoying the beautiful weather, we turned off the main roads occasionally and walked along the edge of the forest. The bodies of frozen French in piles littered the area in all directions. This spectacle already became ordinary and no longer affected us or drew our attention. Suddenly I had the impression that some creature was stirring in the forest near a tree, swaying it. With an automatic curiosity I walked over there and what did I find but a mysterious entity standing on its knees against the pine tree. His attire was the most fantastical and today it would seem amusing. On his head was tied a woman's muff with a scrap of cloth, a woman's jacket dangled from his shoulders, his trousers were all in tatters and showed through so much that there could be no doubt as to the sex of this particular creature. On his feet he only wore the shafts of his boots, wrapped with straw through which his bare toes could be seen. This half-human clutched a small crucifix in his hands, his stare was dull and motionless but his lips were moving subtly. It was evident that he was praying and undoubtedly felt death approaching. For a long time already we were indifferent to all kinds of suffering and death,[43] but the prayer of this soldier dying in the snow of a foreign country had some extraordinarily touching quality. I called over several soldiers and asked the dying man about a few things but he could not tell me anything, the severe cold and hunger having deprived him of his senses and understanding. We picked him up and moved him to a sleigh, wrapped him up as best we could and gave him a drink or two of rum. Then, wishing on a miracle, we brought him to our camp for the night. He was still alive but had to be taken by hand out of the sleigh, into the house and set down. There a new dose of rum revived his ability to speak. He spoke in German with a weak voice and somehow explained to us that he was a captain, Swiss, had served in the 32nd Regiment and other military details.[44] We fed him and no one in the world could have seen such enthusiasm come from a few spoonsful of bad soup. He was examined and fortunately it appeared that he had not spent enough time exposed to lose anything to frostbite. An extreme exhaustion from hunger would have been the cause of his death. All of our comrades gathered the next day to give him clothes and we were forced to take him with us

---

43   Zotov's note: 'For example, G*** K*** [Golenishchev-Kutuzov?] ordered that in our bivouacs we lay out a few frozen French bodies under our heads and along the windward sides for shelter. It did not at all seem strange or terrible at the time'.

44   Both the *32e Régiment de Ligne* and *Lègére* were in Spain during the 1812 campaign. Perhaps the officer was describing previous service, Zotov was misremembering, or a typo was made in publication. Jules du Camp, *Histoire de l'Armée et de tout les Régiments* (Paris: A. Barbier, 1850), Vol.4, pp.xxix-xliii. [Jules du Camp, *History of the Army and all its Regiments* (Paris: A. Barbier, 1850), Vol. 4, pp.xxiv-xliii.]

to the first departure of a large detachment of prisoners heading into the interior of Russia. What happened to him from then, none of us could know. God grant that our assistance helped to return him to his friends and family.

Letting Chichagov's army go ahead, we did not at all march with a military bearing. Every night we were placed in villages, sleeping in warm cabins, ate well, and often even drank until we were merry. Our military activities were limited to collecting prisoners along the way and this work had proved the most peaceful. They were glad to surrender, because they knew they would eat again and maybe even be clothed and shod. Our army did not advance any further than we did. The frosts were ten times stronger than we could hope to be, and from the Berezina to the Niemen more than 60,000 of the enemy perished without firing a shot!

Soon we learned that Napoleon reached Paris and left behind the miserable ruins of his enormous army to fate. He entrusted it to Murat (King of Naples), but he too followed his master's example. Eugene (Viceroy of Italy) became the commander in chief and proved his great ability, bringing the pitiable remnants to the Elbe without any more significant losses.

Either because of the strong frosts or the slow recovery of my wounds, my general health became very poor at this time and I was sent to rest and undergo treatment in Vilno. On November 28th [December 10th], the city was liberated by General Czaplic and the Colonels Seslavin and Tettenborn. I left my *druzhina* but did not know that it would be forever!

In a sleigh and followed by a batman, I rode to the ancient capital of Lithuania, and this two-day journey gave me the opportunity to see so many new episodes of the French retreat, that recalling the memory makes me shiver. Both the physical and moral condition of these unfortunate soldiers surpassed every expectation and defied description. In every home where I stopped to warm up, as the frost was still at its most cruel, I found a pile of the dead and most of them were arranged around the sunken hearths. Frostbitten feet, hands, noses and ears – the sufferers, not knowing the mysteries of the northern climate, scoured the affected areas with snow and rushed to warm them up at the fire; they immediately became gangrenous or suffered a apoplectic shock – and the unfortunates, instead of finding salvation at the fireside, would be killed by it. Others wandered the roads like ghosts, not knowing where they were headed or why. I asked many of them where they were going and they all answered 'to Vilno!' But why? 'The Emperor is there!' I would tell them they were mistaken, that Russians had returned to the city and that their Emperor fled to Paris. They incredulously shook their heads and continued on their way, usually in the opposite direction of their supposed destination. No one thought to collect them all as prisoners of war. They wandered very comfortably between the Russian columns and never engaged them.

I finally reached Vilno and came to the commandant with my papers from the colonel. He shook his head. 'To be treated here!' he exclaimed, and told me it was a bad idea. Everything there, both the people and their homes, was contaminated by the interned French. 'I won't put you in the hospital; they're dying there by the hundreds from a fever. With the locals you're unlikely to find good care and hospitality. All of them give us dirty looks but keep mum and make like they're happy to please'. I answered that I wished to be placed with one of the common people, from whom my modesty and most moderate requests would not inspire resentment. 'Well enough! I will send you to the Petersburg suburb where it's quieter. Still, be careful. At the first sign of some kind of scheme, notify me immediately'. I bowed and rode to my new home. It was outside the city and almost in the middle of the suburb to the right of the main road. The home was clean and well lit, which convinced me of the good spiritual qualities of my hosts, as one typically followed the other. The owner met me and my quartering certificate very coolly. It was a false impression however, as he was glad. I was not given special chambers, but was put up in a large common room and when my host asked me about food and drink, I replied that I was no perfectionist and would accept whatever they would serve me. My answer smoothed his worried forehead. Looking around carefully and not bothering anyone with my questions, I saw that my master was a merchant of a minor status. He was a widower and had two daughters – and had only just been rid of a few Russian guests two days before my arrival. Was it any wonder that the arrival of a new tenant did not excite him? He was depressed and un-talkative but did not seem to show any sign of ill-will, even beginning to talk to me after dinner. Being by nature averse to conversation, I did not push him far and our political discussions ended with a humble yes and no.

I made far more progress in getting to know his daughters. It has been known since the creation of the world that there is always some kind of innate sympathy between officers and their hosts' daughters. It develops easiest with Polish girls, is improved with the French, and one reaches graduation with the German women. Unfortunately, I was the most inexperienced officer in the whole Russian Army in that department, and very shy and timid with all of my campaign hostesses, which according to military logic were always supposed to be an accessory of an officer's lodgings. I managed to learn immediately that the older daughter's name was Barbara and the younger was Jozefa. The older was more beautiful, more cheery, more outgoing, and perhaps more experienced. The younger was shy, timid, pock-marked, and pensive. A 17-year-old officer covered in various wounds was a rather interesting subject for the girls and they both looked on me rather affectionately. At first I also gave them affectionate glances and tiny sighs but then I made up my mind on which to turn my affections, and my decision was for the younger. Many might burst out laughing at this choice, but consider it. Jozefa better matched my character, while the liveliness and gaiety of the older soldier amazed and intimidated me. Barbara soon noticed my preference and rather than take offense, she began to help me, mocked me for my timidity and scolded her sister for her silence. The father always slept until the afternoon and during that time we stayed in my room alone. The hours flew quickly and joyfully. But… *honi soit qui mal y pense*,[45] I do not mean to offend or fuel the imagination for those hours. I was an absolute Molchalin with my Sofiya there in that room. 'What do you think we were doing? … He held my hand to my heart, from the depth of his soul he sighed – not a word was loosed!'[46] I don't know if my companion was secretly glad that fate had sent her such a timid and inexperienced admirer, but I remember them constantly laughing among themselves and whispering, but pride would not admit that it was at my expense and my unbearable shyness insisted that it was impossible to act any differently. Naturally my 17-year-old's imagination often drew a much more pleasant image than reality, which led to very long conversations and passionate tirades that made me conscious of my listeners and how my clever phrases and enthusiasms repeated themselves in a betraying fashion until embarrassment welled in my chest. At that point I would postpone until the next day but then repeat myself as before.

My appointment to that home in the suburb was very beneficial to me due to the fever raging in the city at the time, which passed from the hospitals to the private homes. Up to 15,000 French had passed through Vilno during their retreat. Most died from incurably advanced illnesses which were passed on to the residents. Every day carts carried the dead outside the city to bury them at a safe distance. My illness had no consequence and was almost past after a week of rest and good food. But this time I was not eager or in a hurry to return to the army. Either because military affairs were no longer attractive to me or because the frost had dampened the ardour of my youth, I was determined to live with my hosts as long as I could. Perhaps Jozefa was also a motivating factor behind that desire, as we both became gradually more outgoing and talkative the longer we spent together.

Although no one would notice whether a certain ensign made a timely recovery or not, my conscience compelled me to report to the commandant that I almost completely felt healthy and then asked permission to stay in Vilno for another week. He readily agreed and asked if I was satisfied with my host. He did not inquire about the host's daughters and instead ordered me to be careful in dealing with the locals. I returned to Barbara and Jozefa with a content heart and a glowing smile.

My reclusive life soon bored me. I ran about the city, observing its buildings, institutions and neighbourhoods and began to look for friends. During wartime, I

---

45   Anglo-Norman for 'Shame on whoever thinks badly of it'. It is the motto of the British Order of the Garter.

46   '…His eyes never strayed from mine!' In Alexandr Griboyedov's comedy *Woe from Wit*, the characters Molchalin and Sofiya spend their nights in a pure kind of courtly love, which Zotov quotes from Sofiya's lines in Act 1, Scene 5. It is later revealed however that Molchalin is only keeping up appearances for the sake of his position as the secretary to Sofiya's father. With the parlour maid, Liza, he is far less chivalrous. Александр Грибоедов, *Горе от Ума* (St Petersburg: Типография П А. Кулиша, 1862), p.16. [Alexandr Griboyedov, *Woe from Wit* (St. Petersburg: Press of P. A. Kulish, 1862), p.16].

could always find them and with them I began to gradually replace Jozefa, sometimes snubbing her for an entire day. Such short walks continued and I paid dearly for them however. The commandant was correct. When visiting some friends living in the city, I never paid attention to the faces of their hosts. My comrades did not have my vice of timidity and their hosts frequently looked at us in a most disapproving fashion. But for a Russian, none of that is of any consequence. We made fun of them, bullied them, pestered their wives and daughters and in such a mood we often hopped from the lodgings of one friend to another in the same night. One night when it was particularly dark and the lights in Vilno were woefully inadequate, we were greeted on the street by several gunshots but from whom or whence it could not be known and the darkness made catching our attackers impossible. Likewise, they failed to hit us. We of course drew our sabres and closed together, setting off at a brisk pace to the nearest *Hauptwacht*. There we were given an escort and returned to our homes peacefully. The next day, I had to report to the commandant about everything that had transpired. It seemed that such events were not rare, and without any evidence to pursue, the matter was ended – so too did my evening walks. I reasoned that it was much healthier and beneficial to remain shy at home with Jozefa than to brave the night against shadowy gunmen.

That incident made me seriously think about returning to the army. I announced my desire to the commandant and he told me that I would be informed when I was free to leave the day before my departure. The private soldiers recuperating in the hospitals from all the regiments were to be grouped together and assigned two or three officers according to circumstances and then assigned marching routes to re-join the army. The senior officer was always naturally the leader of the group to which he was assigned and it sometimes occurred that this commanding officer fancied himself the absolute master of every village they passed through, acting the despot. There was an unfortunate example of one such partisan being subjected to the full severity of court-martial because when passing each Polish magnate's estate, he stole everything that caught his fancy, even their womenfolk.

Learning of my imminent departure, Jozefa and Barbara became sad, their father much more affectionate, and I a little bolder. After our brief meetings failed to be enough for me, I started to pursue long into the evening. One night, Barbara tired of my boring subjects and went to bed, leaving me alone with Jozefa. Alone indeed!

The next morning, when I got up, she was not even in the house. Her brutal father sent her somewhere, to an aunt or some other relation. For what, I did not know. Barbara told me in confidence I was guilty for it all, and no matter how I swore to her of my physical and spiritual innocence, she laughed and refused to believe me. I was very annoyed because I would rather no one knew about it. After two days, I was on the march and I parted with my beloved Vilno, which I never saw again.

I was accompanied by an officer from our *druzhina* whom I will refer to only as Lieutenant V. He was the head of a detachment for collecting recuperated men of the lower ranks. The team consisted of a hundred men from various regiments and we all travelled together. We were assigned a route along a road which the main army did not take, and this was more suitable for all the comforts of life. My comrade, an old army veteran, had his own logic for life on the march. It seemed the law only applied to his hard earned property, and the rights of other people's did not concern him. At first I felt it was my duty to remind him of the grave consequences of such a way of thinking but he answered me in a very friendly way that I was still too young to judge the situation and that he alone would be responsible for everything. I gradually became silently pleased with his orders. Soon I unfortunately noticed that my philanthropy really was out of place. Either the residents were accustomed to the autocratic methods of the military detachments, or their aversion to Russian people was the cause, but when the detachment arrived for night lodgings, the people very calmly said that they had nothing to feed the men. With the very same tone, my lieutenant always answered: 'good! We'll find it ourselves'. He then began searching all the nooks and crannies of their homes as if he knew them already. He immediately found the pantry, broke the lock and would always find very abundant provisions of every sort. Then of course he would take more than we needed, though it was necessary to stock up. Two or three wagons with the detachment were always needed, for the bundles of equipment and the other recreational weaknesses. The officers also added one for themselves so that they did not carry anything while they walked, but each day there was a story with this baggage train. In the village where the detachment settled for the night, all the horses disappeared, the owners having ridden off with them into the woods. Such action was in accordance with my comrade's logic. He did not release the hired horses until more could be obtained on the journey and the drivers nearly always fled beforehand. Each time, the horses became the property of the lieutenant by virtue of being the 'closest and legitimate living heir'. When some helpful Jews revealed to us where best to steal horses from the other residents, a portion of the detachment set off into the woods and along the footpaths in search of the hidden horses, caught them and led them back to the commander. This too naturally became his property.

Our route would take us through Troki, Kovno, Insterburg, and Wehlau to Königsberg, but as my comrade altogether hated the city where we were ceremoniously prescribed our quarters and the courteous coldness of its residents, giving us few occasions to take in the sights within, we stopped at every village we came across, sometimes resting for a whole day (or two, or three). Reaching the Niemen in such a fashion, we decided not to cross it through Kovno but through the village of Shlinovo, 15 *versta*s [16 km] upriver. There we found a detachment like ours which had stayed in the village for more than a week and was going to depart the next day. The officers lived with the local Prussian forest commissioner and we managed to squeeze ourselves in too. They told us many good things about the locals' hospitality that we were excited and gave us the desire to stay longer than usual.

The forester had (again) two daughters, the younger of which was sick and at her bedside inseparably sat her husband, a noble of some kind, resident of the same village and modestly endowed with arable farmland of his own, but the elder sister, Annchen, was a wonderful girl. Her father was a widowed old man and could not handle finances, so she had long ruled over the whole household. All the officers quartered there naturally followed behind her all day and made fun of each other for their failed advances. Being new in love affairs, they elected to send me to avenge them, and I was pleased to accept this assignment, all the while knowing that it was beyond my abilities and that my damned timidity and inexperience would not serve me very well in that grand endeavour. Squandering a whole night, we were left alone the next morning with the village elders, the forester and his daughters. I immediately gained their respect since I could speak German. In the eyes of the old Prussian, it was my primary virtue. He most of all loved the German language, politics, wine, and money. All of that occupied me very little; I was far more interested in Annchen. Although by the logic of my Lieutenant V, she must be considered his property, he very graciously conceded her to me when he saw how I always melted at the sight of her and went to one of the other homes to seek his entertainment, but returning to his headquarters with strict punctuality for breakfast, lunch, tea, and dinner.

While staying in that village, we heard about the first defections of Napoleon's allies. The Prussian General Yorck separated from Macdonald and concluded a convention of neutrality with Russia and first gave Europe an example of a general commanding the political participation of his forces without the consent of his sovereign.[47] The consequences justified his actions. Yorck's convention spread confidence everywhere that a general peace would be concluded soon and the rumour excited everyone's hearts. For us and our lieutenant too, he served as the most indisputable pretext for remaining in the village until the publication of peace and further orders, rather than continue our properly scheduled advance.

We lived in Shlinovo for over two weeks. It was a most agreeable time for me. The love of Annchen made this tiny village into a charming El Dorado for me. And – though no one believes it – our love was platonic. Due to my shyness, she first had to encourage me and then I became bolder and more adventurous. And there, as in Vilno, her sister, having recovered, was a great assistance to me and advised me on a decisive attack, but I continuously postponed it and enjoyed a more morally sound relationship. Often we rode with Annchen to Kovno and she bought me everything imaginable (with their own money, I ashamedly admit), and

---

47   Lieutenant General Ludwig Yorck made his unauthorized peace at Taurrogen on 18 [30] December, 1812 with Major General Karl von Diebitsch und Narten (Ivan Ivanovich Dibich) representing Russia. Ward et al., *Cambridge Modern History*, Vol. 9, p.505.; Andreyevskiy et al., *Brockhaus and Efron Dictionary*, s.v. 'Тауроген.' [Andreyevskiy et al., *Brockhaus and Efron Dictionary*, s.v. 'Tauroggen.']

I was delighted like a child with her amazing surprises. But despite my shyness, we both often felt that, my being 17 and her being 19, God only knows it would be right for us to end our relationship on a positive note, if even with a single event, to ensure that it would end on the highest terms possible and not suddenly turn sour – a fact of which I am still ashamed to this day.

Instigated by her sister, my operatic love and her own feelings, Annchen finally decided to grant me a romantic encounter. The place of our rendezvous was to be her sister's bedroom, one hour after her father and his company retired to their chambers. One could imagine my excitement, my happiness, my eager anticipation! Truthfully, during these pleasant feelings, an involuntary fear tightened around my chest and squeezed out my breath, but I attributed it to the impatience of an enamoured man preparing for such an important step in his life. After spending the whole night conversing spiritedly about politics with the old man, I finally brought him to yawning. We bid each other good night and then we parted. I slept in the same room as the lieutenant, but since I did not divulge my date to anyone, I waited until he fell asleep. I knew that he would not keep me waiting for long. Indeed in only ten minutes he announced with a resounding voice that he would sleep the sleep of heroes. Snuffing the candle, I sank into the very sweetest of daydreams and rebuked the lethargic pendulum, whose monotonous ticking was particularly slow that night. We always retired at 10. Theoretically I had to wait until the clock struck 11. Such boredom! The whole cosmorama of my fantasies already passed before my eyes several times until the images became confused and disconnected. I sought out new materials but the swirling in my head was too chaotic. Little by little however, I brought my dreams to their proper systematic order. I felt warm, comfortable and calm. With an imagined indifference, I waited hours for the fateful battle – and continued to wait with a philosophical patience – and when I came to my senses, it was morning.

Such was my first experience! I slept like a Russian *bogatyr* through the whole night. I probably fell asleep from the very beginning of my vigil and all of my vivid expectations and daydreams were actual dreams. What a horrible awakening! I did not dare stir. I wanted to feign illness but suddenly heard the voice of the lieutenant, who treated me to a morning conversation. I did not really pay him my full attention until he began to ask me questions and courtesy demanded a response from me, but I answered infrequently and at random. He managed to lift me out of my despair a little however. To hide my shame, I begged the lieutenant to resume our march immediately.

'God be with you, what a thought!' he answered. 'We're well enough where we are. The Army isn't doing anything. And your dearly beloved is here…' All the conviction in his eloquence was in vain. I did not relent, and, since he had a sincere affection and respect for me despite his seniority, he sighed and said: 'alright! Have it your way. Tomorrow morning we march!' With those words, he whistled to his batman and ordered him to deliver to the sergeant major the order to prepare for a speech. In my dumbstruck relief, I rushed up and hugged him.

Soon the whole house was roused and everyone met with the father in his bedroom as he was drinking his coffee. Like a convicted criminal, I appeared before Annchen and took her off to the side and told her my prepared lie. With unfeigned tears born of shame, I told her of our departure the next day and that I was so shocked and so affected by it like a lunatic, that I did not know what to do all night for the anguish. My revelation was unexpected. She burst into tears and announced it to her family through sobs. They were all surprised and disappointed, even the old man himself. Although he loved his money, which our sojourn had frustrated badly, he had become so accustomed with us in our two weeks that it was as if we were family and the separation was very painful for him.

Everyone came to the lieutenant with questions about the cause for such a speedy departure but only received the laconic answer of: 'that's how it has to be! We march tomorrow!' The whole day was spent in mourning tears, embraces, assurances of eternal fidelity, and on the next day, we were beyond the frontiers of Russia.

It was an altogether new feeling for me. Coming to the defence of the fatherland, humiliated by the audacious invasion of all the forces of Europe, I never imagined then that in less than six months, we would cross the Niemen and petition for the freedom of other peoples. Before the appearance of Russian forces beyond the Niemen and Vistula, the whole of Europe, deceived by the bulletins of the French Army, never believed the particular rumours spread about the complete destruction of that gigantic assemblage of arms trekking through Russia. Even the famous 29th Bulletin spoke of small losses suffered by the Grand Armée,[48] but the appearance of the Russians and the miserable handfuls of retreating Frenchmen under Eugene tore the bandages from the eyes of the blinded people.[49] Swears and curses rained down from all sides on Napoleon in his novel defeat. Those people enslaved by his ambition rattled their chains with impatient rage and Prussia was the first to embark on a last, desperate effort to restore her political independence. Weakened by perennial disasters and humiliations, Prussia felt that success in the struggle with Napoleon required tremendous, desperate efforts from all the classes of her nation and that the misfortunes responsible for its political insignificance would be overturned in the coming war and she would be cast the exasperated victor. But in such moments, the fate of a people develops the true strength and character of it citizens. Prussia endured that ordeal with such hardships, such sacrifices, and

---

48   The 29th Bulletin of the Grand Army, dated 21 November [3 December], 1812, was the first public admission of defeat by Napoleon, but attributed its destruction primarily to the weather. The destruction of such an army, regardless of who deserved the credit or blame, could not practically be hidden from the public. Georges de Chambray, *Histoire de l'Expédition de Russie* (Paris: Pillet, 1825), Vol.3, pp.209-217. [Georges de Chambray, *History of the Russian Expedition* (Paris: Pillet, 1825), Vol.3, pp.209-217.]

49   Eugène de Beauharnais, Viceroy of Italy, assumed command on 5 [17] January, 1813, in the absence of first Napoleon and then Joachim Murat, King of Naples, as mentioned above. Ward et al., *Cambridge Modern History*, Vol. 9, p.511.

such glory that the descendants of that generation could never hope to exceed the exploits of their fathers. How strong and majestic was that proclamation of the King to his subjects![50] He did not conceal any of the upcoming difficulties or unavoidable casualties, but on the basis of faith in Providence and out of love for the people, he aroused a noble audacity in every class to the celebrated cause: the liberation of the fatherland. Thus commenced a new era in Prussia's existence.

Perhaps my judgement and praise for the Prussians will seem biased. I confess this predilection. It remains with me from that great epoch. Future historians will very calmly discuss those events in Europe in their offices, but whoever was not an eyewitness will not be able to produce a true image of them. The most notable, the most powerful and the heaviest element for the historical narrative must be the spirit which animated all the classes of the people. Who would believe now that the same phlegmatic Germans, whose politics are a mug of beer, at that time ran about with such an enthusiasm, their soldiers screaming, their bards chanting rapturous songs; all flew to the River Spree to die for the freedom of Prussia.

Perhaps one of the reasons for my attachment to the Prussians is that they received us with such warmth and tenderness and were so obliging that the memory of them will always warm me with a pleasant feeling. After passing through the scorn and ill-will of other peoples, to reach those who considered you their deliverer and are pleased to share their homes with you is a pleasure that is much easier to feel than to convey.

That entire land, the whole lifestyle of its residents, their population, industry and education – after the smoky cabins of Lithuania, after the terrible and backward peasantry of Samogitia, after all the poverty and idleness – to cross into Prussia will inevitably make one biased in their favour. In the village of Shlinovo where we stayed for two weeks we found the gentle family of the Prussian *Forstmeister*, and now at every step, each home that took us in was tenfold better.

Insterburg was the first Prussian city that I saw and we decided to rest there for a day. We were showered with affection and entertainment. The whole town gathered at our host's home to hear my stories about the campaign, the Berezina, the frosts, and the French Army's catastrophe. They were surprised and touched by my eloquence in German. I was humbled by the occasional doubt of my claimed Russian origin, but I confidently assured them that all Petersburg officers spoke German well.

On the first night I was shocked by what was given to me to sleep. It was a down feather mattress, which really should have been worn as a coat. In vain I

---

50   The proclamation 'To My People', published 20 March, 1813, called upon all classes and ethnicities within Prussia to fight against Napoleon and was unprecedented in Prussian history for defining and justifying the state's policy to the general public. Friedrich Wilhelm III, 'An Mein Volk', *Schlesische Privilegirte Zeitung*, 20 March, 1813. [Friedrich Wilhelm III, 'To My People', *The Silesian Privileged Newspaper*, 20 March, 1813].

asked for a simple blanket but the maid told me that such bedding was only in the villages. That was reason enough and I gave up on the issue, drowning myself in the waves of down and falling asleep, conceding that the sybaritic pleasure was very comfortable. Subsequently, I became used to the luxury and now in my old age when I reminisce,[51] I am saddened that such down covers are not in fashion.

From that town I wrote my first letter abroad. How gaily I bragged in my writing! But who in their youth did not embellish on their exploits? I remember however that despite inflating my tale, I was rather modest in my descriptions.

We travelled from Insterburg to Wehlau. On the 6th [18th] of February, after a severe winter, came an early spring. Larks were singing in the fields and the peasants already began to work their lands. For a Petersburgian confident in the constancy of his climate, the appearance of the spring in the beginning of February was both delightful and fascinating.

I wrote earlier that the route given to us was from Vilno to Wehlau and Königsberg, but we travelled so slowly the whole while that I did not know at the time that the military route had already changed. Printed announcements reported that detachments in transit would, instead of Wehlau, move through Allenburg, Preußisch-Holland, and Eylau to reach Marienburg on the Vistula. I do not know if the lieutenant read them, but only that he did not consider himself responsible for changing our route. We calmly entered Wehlau. This gave rise to a very unpleasant incident about which I am still angry, despite my fondness for the Prussians.

Our detachment always took some wagons from one transit to the next (which was no difficulty during our stay in Prussia), and we, along with the lieutenant and a soldier-quartermaster, always marched with one in front until we stopped at our lodgings around dinnertime. We reached Wehlau in the very same fashion. Truthfully we had spoken at the prior lodgings about how all the detachments were to be rerouted through Allenburg instead, but my lieutenant did not want to know about it [and feigned ignorance in favour of our present course]. Marching, we assigned a small detachment to them for the day and by noon we reached a village, occupied the best house, and demanded the village *Schulz* come to us and announced to him that he had to accommodate a hundred men and two officers with food and quarters for two days.[52] The man scratched his head and raising his hat for a moment that felt eternal and replied that he could give us neither because of an order from the civil magistrate which confined the passage of soldiers through the appointed Allenburg.

'What nonsense!' shouted the lieutenant. 'Your magistrate orders you, not me. I have a marching route from the Commandant of Vilno and I'm not changing it

---

51 Zotov was 41 years old when his *Stories of the Campaigns of 1812 and 1813* were first published in 1836.

52 A 'Schulz', 'Schulze' or 'Schultheiß' was the village elder, mayor, or sheriff. Today, the word is a common surname. John Ebers ed., *The New and Complete Dictionary of the German and English Languages* (Leipzig: Britkopf and Haertel, 1799), s.v. 'Schultheis, der'.

by the will of your magistrate. Give us quarters and provisions or we'll take it for ourselves'.

As the translator, I conveyed all of this to the *Schulz*, softening it as much as I could, but he replied that he could not accommodate us and advised us to go to the *Bürgermeister* in Wehlau proper, who alone could order him to help us. He ordered the peasants not to give us anything and asserted his authority upon us. My lieutenant became enraged and, without any further ado, punched him on the cheek so hard that his hat flew off and he nearly tumbled down after it. The *Schulz* quite calmly picked up his hat and said that the gentleman-officer will be held responsible for his actions and that neither quarters nor provisions would be given whatsoever. Groups of peasants gathered around us and although their faces expressed a respectful confusion, the speech of their elder proposing to send us to the town began to worry them. I hurried to translate every word of the elder to my lieutenant and he reasoned that until the detachment arrived, we ought to hold our ground in a defensive position.

In that fashion, pushing our way through the crowd around us like a Russian does, we cleared the path to the home we selected for ourselves. We locked the gate and all the doors and reinforced the entrance with the quartermaster. We decided to wait out their siege and repel any assault, should it have come to that. Sitting by an unlocked window, we watched all the movements of our new enemies but did not see any strong preparation to attack. The crowds of peasants paced back and forth and gossiped amongst each other. We could clearly hear everything they said – they all blamed the stubbornness of the *Schulz* and were prepared to bring us what we requested. It would be some time before the rest of our detachment arrived and the lieutenant was looking forward to it, threatening to take offensive action when they did. I urged him as much as I could that he should travel with me to the town to meet with the mayor, who could truly not refuse hospitality to Russian soldiers, and the lieutenant nearly agreed with this measure of caution. At first, he wanted to see what the *Schulz* would do with his dishevelled hat. Suddenly the crowd in the street seemed to grow larger and the elder leading them had at some point changed into a green uniform and a tricorne with a plume. Pausing before the windows, they demanded to be let in. By order of our lieutenant, I announced to them that they could speak from where they were. After consulting among themselves, the *Schulz* asked us to admit the *Weginspektor* (an inspector of the roads) into the house for negotiating with us. The lieutenant agreed and the private went to the gate, opened it, and held his musket at the charge before calling in the esteemed Prussian officer. Our fears were unfounded, as no one tried to follow behind him. The gate was locked after him however and it seemed to quite worry the Prussian. Appearing before us, he very grandly and at length began to speak to us about admitting our detachment, the principles of discipline, and the friendship between the King of Prussia and the Emperor of Russia.

'He'll be talking this rot for a full hour', my lieutenant exclaimed impatiently. He only asked of him: 'can you give us quarters and provisions here?' and I translated it.

'No', replied the inspector rather coldly.

'Well then, tell them to go to hell! We'll stay where we are and whatever they don't give voluntarily, we'll take for ourselves'. I translated his words for the inspector.

'For this violence, you will be taking on a large responsibility', continued the Prussian, and again began a long tirade about the duties of men in war.

'Ask him thoroughly, brother, who he is, what rank he holds and by what right he's come to teach us his worldviews'. The gentleman *Weginspektor* very proudly described to me his position: he was an inspector of roads and very humbly added that he was also *almost* an officer.

As soon as the lieutenant learned this, he flew into a rabid rage. 'You son of a bitch! This little non-com dares to teach me what's what, dares to sit down with me (ignoring that we invited him first)! Get out of here right now, otherwise, I'll order you a *hundert* blows with the flat of the blade, Russian style!' This I did not translate; the Prussian could understand for himself by the lieutenant's gestures and tone of voice. He left the room with haste, unlocked the gate by the billeted soldier, shut it behind himself and retreated back into the noisy crowd. Now the voice of the *Schulz* was supported by the semi-officer and both demanded the peasants to assist in forcibly send us to the town.

Suddenly at the end of the street came the sound of a trumpet (in our detachment was a single cavalry trumpeter who substituted the role of a drummer with his instrument). Our men had arrived and entered the village with a great importance and brought order to the crowds. The lieutenant jumped with joy. 'Now we'll show all these rascals!' he shouted, ordered the gate be unlocked and rushed out onto the street. I followed him, begging him to be careful. 'Oh, brother, don't fear! We'll show them how Russians make an entrance...'

'But for God's sake don't be violent', I said.

'Be quiet!'

He immediately drew the men up into a formation for battle and ordered that the *Schulz* and *Weginspektor* come forward. They appeared and with them came a small group of peasants, who stopped at a respectful distance from us. The lieutenant himself demanded for two wagons and asked if he could get them voluntarily or if he needed to take them by force. The *Schulz* ordered the wagons to be prepared in a quarter of an hour.

'And now', said the lieutenant, 'I am taking both of you, the *Schulz* and this *Unteroffizier*, under arrest until we reach the *Bürgermeister* to file a complaint that one of you has denied accommodations and provisions to Russian soldiers and the other has aroused the peasantry to violence against us'.

They both became flustered. 'Under arrest!? Only by the authority of His Majesty the King of Prussia can we be arrested...'

'Your attention please', answered the lieutenant. 'This is not a case for you to judge whether I'm right or wrong. Look at what I have at my disposal and see for yourselves'. He pointed at the menacing looking detachment as he spoke. 'Then choose for yourselves: do you want to come voluntarily as prisoners with me into town or do you want to be tied up and dragged there?'

Neither of them liked that very much. They addressed the peasants, demanding their protection, but the crowd would not budge and told them to go willingly into the town. They had no recourse but to submit to their fate. The wagons arrived and we sat on one with the lieutenant and the two prisoners were put on the other with a pair of burly cavalry troopers to guard them. The detachment instructed a sergeant major to stand watch under arms in the street of the village until we returned. Finally we departed for Wehlau and appeared before the mayor.

I described the whole incident to him in the most resplendent German phrases but diplomacy reached an impasse. He could not officially allow a military detachment, contrary to the newly promulgated orders, to pass by a different route, but he also could not allow, given the present political situation, to see a detachment of Russian soldiers including the wounded to be denied hospitality. However, he found a way out of this contradictory dilemma. Both of our prisoners were called forward. The inspector received a severe reprimand and was then released, while the *Schulz* was ordered to provide our detachment with provisions for that day and the next (the lieutenant having announced that we needed a day's rest). We asked the mayor to admit us to Allenburg after the day's rest, according to the newly assigned military route. The lieutenant demanded that a written announcement of his orders be given. It was given immediately and we rode with the *Schulz* back to his village. Thus, as the proverb says: the wolves were fed and the sheep were safe. The detachment was still standing under arms. We called for an assembly of the villagers and announced the *Bürgermeister*'s decision as it was written. The *Schulz* was forced to confirm its validity and in half an hour we all became the best of friends with the inhabitants.

Making merry there for two days, we departed according to the new route and everywhere we arrived received us willingly. There were no other incidents or anything noteworthy to recall for the duration of the march to Marienburg. Only Preußisch-Eylau held me up for a day. Six years had passed since the famous battle on those fields, and how the political makeup of Europe had changed in that time! (I did not foresee that in a little more than a year there would be even more surprising upheavals). I took some time to walk around and see all the neighbourhoods, in addition to the famous cemetery where Napoleon's headquarters were situated during the battle and where a number of Russians crept up in a snowstorm, just barely missing the chance to capture him.[53] No remarkable signs of the

53 The battle of Eylau was fought on the 26-27 January [7-8 February], 1807. The historian Mikhaylovskiy-Danilevskiy attested that a single Russian battalion came within a hundred paces of Napoleon in the

battle remained for me to observe. Even much of the population did not know the details of the battle. The fate of the Prussian monarchy was hanging in the balance then, but the citizens of Eylau remember it now somewhat indifferently. Such a feeling in the present weakens and destroys the memories of the past!

Finally we reached the destination of our march. We stood on the banks of the Vistula at Marienburg. Appearing before the commandant, we received an order to relinquish the detachment and remain in quarters provided until further notice. The detachments being sent out of the city were not a hundred-strong, but a thousand. On that same day, we learned that all of our militia had assembled in Marienburg and set out down the Vistula to the siege of Danzig. I rushed to find my *druzhina* but it remained back at the border in Jurburg.[54] Consequently, I was orphaned. The commandant gave me a choice: either I march with a detachment in the main army, where I would be properly assigned to some regiment, or I would report to General Adadurov, commanding the St. Petersburg Militia, who would assign me to a different *druzhina*. The third option was to return to Jurburg. I strongly abhorred the third option and chose the second. I had already seen battle, but I wanted to experience the pleasure of a siege. Whether I chose well or poorly, I did not know. With the regular army, however, I probably would have prospered better in the service.

The next morning, I appeared before General Adadurov and was received very affectionately. He immediately assigned me to the 5th *Druzhina*, which was at that time commanded by Collegiate Assessor Semyon Nikolayevich Korsakov, due to all his seniors being sick or wounded.[55] I have just written that I would have prospered more in the army, but I must admit however with gratitude that in the company of officers I found myself, I could hardly have done better. I found myself in a completely new world. In the previous officer corps, I felt the advantage of education, but now it vanished and without any humiliation to my vanity. Previously I had enjoyed universal respect but was alone, while now everyone around me belonged to the single sphere of the finest society. What a difference I saw then between a student and those enlightened people. Everyone knew as much as I did and nobody thought to remind me of it. Any ostentation fell before the subtle sarcastic quips of high society. I consider the time spent in that company

cemetery, but he could not name the regiment to which it belonged. Александр Михайловский-Данилевский, *Описание Второй Войны Императора Александра с Наполеоном в 1806 и 1807 годах* (St. Petersburg: Штаб Отдельного Корпуса Внутренней Стражи, 1846), *pp.*190-197. [Aleksandr Mikhaylovskiy-Danilevskiy, *Description of the Second War between Emperor Alexander and Napoleon in the years 1806 and 1807* (St Petersburg: Staff of the Independent Corps of the Interior Guard, 1846) pp.190-197.]

54 Zotov's original unit, the 14th *Druzhina*, had been garrisoned in Jurburg since 7 [19] December, 1812. Steinheil, *Notes Regarding the St. Petersburg Militia*, Vol. 1, p.204.

55 Collegiate assessor was Grade VIII in the civil service, equal to a major in the army. Shepelyov, *Titles, Uniforms and Orders*, pp.117-118, 154.

to be the most pleasant and beneficial in my life. The honesty of that whole corps gave each man his due justice and that made me even more proud that I belonged to such an aristocratic assembly.

A few days later, we reached Danzig.

III

It was the end of February. We travelled to Dirschau. I, being able to speak German, went on ahead with the quarters-officers. Another officer accompanied me and of course we immediately became friends. Could you imagine that one of these modest quarters-officers would eventually become a famous writer and a great honour to our literature and our age? He was M.N. Zagoskin![56] At the time, he did not think at all about his future writings. That passion and ability evolved in him after the campaign. Then, he was just a hilarious and witty officer with all the knowledge of a well-educated man. We rode together with him towards our destination outside Danzig and procured quarters for our *druzhina*s together (he belonged to a different one than I, but spent all of his free time with us). Thus by the 25th of February [9th of March], we arrived at Danzig. Our *druzhina* took the village of Klein-Quadendorf, and there we saw for the first time how far the prosperity of a peasant could extend. Our host owned 16 horses, 30 cows, and many stores of provisions which nearly fed all of our *druzhina* with its officers (a mere 136 men in total) for a month, and only after that time did he start to take payment from our treasury as compensation. Such prosperity among the inhabitants was a result of the fact that Danzig and the surrounding lands was a free city since the time of the Peace of Tilsit.[57] In those six years, the population did not pay any taxes and traded without duties, becoming very rich for themselves. This freedom and wealth created a delicate political view of Napoleon. They did not want Danzig to ever fall back under the sceptre of the Prussian King.

And so we stood before Danzig! The militia had to occupy a flooded plain, which was created by the French to secure the weaker flank of the city. Having built a dam on the Vistula, they flooded all the low-lying neighbourhoods. As a result, all the postal communications, guards on the forward outposts, and attacks launched by both sides were conducted in flat-bottomed boats, from which a man could jump out and wade through waist-high water if need be.

---

56 Mikhail Nikolayevich Zagoskin was an immensely popular novelist and playwright in his lifetime and a pioneer of historical fiction in the Russian language. His ability to capture the colloquial speech of different classes and create authentic Russian characters made his works accessible to a broad audience. Andreyevskiy et al., *Brockhaus and Efron Dictionary*, s.v. 'Загоскин, Михаил Николаевич.' [Andreyevskiy et al., *Brockhaus and Efron Dictionary*, s.v. 'Zagoskin, Mikhail Nikolayevich.']

57 The treaty between France and Prussia at Tilsit was signed on 27 June [9 July], 1807. The Franco-Russian treaty was signed two days prior. Ward et al., *Cambridge Modern History*, Vol. 9, p.292.

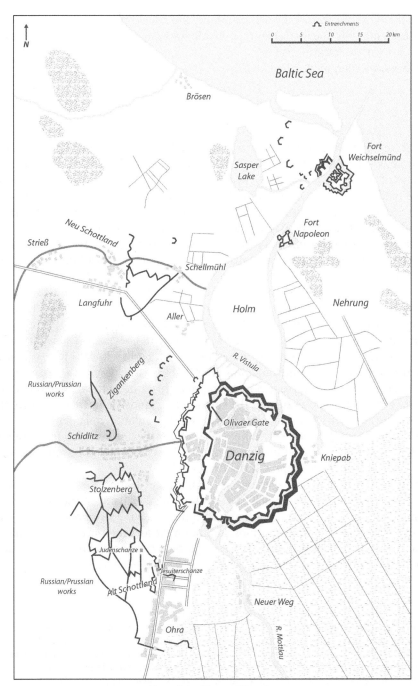

Map of the Siege of Danzig.

Do I need to describe the locations surrounding and reinforcing Danzig? It is all so well known. It was a very moderate city with a population of 60,000 and its neighbourhoods were beautiful but bristling with countless fortifications, built at leisure over the course of six years by Napoleon's best engineers. From the beginning of the siege, we had very little opportunity to see the beauty of its suburbs and cottages. Occupying the flooded lands, we saw only an archipelago of houses and trees emerging from the water, heard only the croaking of frogs and dealt only with the incessant guards and patrols, occasionally exchanging fire with the French boatmen for fun, which was always very surprising for those gathering provisions from house to house. When the militia arrived, the besieging corps was under the command of General Löwis and consisted of 10,000 men.[58] Inside Danzig, across all of its sections, there were more than 30,000 men. We were spread out across 20 *verstas* [12.8 km] and they could send to any point a mass more than ten times stronger, yet all of their relentless attacks ended in our favour.

We sometimes lived very peacefully with the French however. There were many beautiful homes on the flooded plain, which neither we nor they seized, but which we both often visited. At one of them, close to an advance guard maintained by our *druzhina*, lived an old Danzig merchant and his three daughters. Some of us were there almost every day. Arriving one day at an unusual time, we saw another boat tied to the fence. Assuming that it was from some other *druzhina*, we approached the nice home and entered the room. What did we find? Four French officers were melting before the flattery of our beauties. We flew into a rage and drew our sabres, the girls screamed and a duel nearly broke out before the old man suddenly stopped us. In a most touching manner, he urged us not to destroy each other and his home. 'No matter who would win, I will still lose, as both sides hold me responsible for the crime of our warm reception, both the Russians and French. But you may judge for yourself whether I should bear it or another. If there were ever a force posted on this spot, I would of course be compelled to follow the general rules of war and not admit others to it, but now I find myself on some sort of no man's land and regardless of if I wished it, I was obliged to be hospitable to whomever should visit. If you would be so kind, gentlemen, leave behind all your quarrels outside my house and if you want to fight each other, then take it onto the flooded plain. In my opinion, you are better off sitting and visiting with me in peace and friendship. On the field of battle, you will each fulfil your duty and kill each other, but here, what personal quarrels do you have? Take each other's

---

58 Lieutenant General Friedrich von Löwis of Menar commanded the besieging corps at Danzig from 22 January [3 February], 1813 until 11 [23] April when Duke Alexander of Württemberg assumed command. Steinheil, *Notes Regarding the St. Petersburg Militia*, Vol. 2, pp.57-63.

hands and share with me a good Johannisberger'.[59] The Frenchmen laughed at first and then gave us their hands.

'The old man is right!' they cried. 'He always is!' Silently we lowered our sabres and took the hands of the French. In half an hour, we were conversing with them amicably as though we were close friends. Not a word was said regarding politics. We promised each other not to tell anyone about our meeting and, as long as we were on the flooded plain, no one learned about it. We continued to meet the old man and his daughters but very rarely did we ever again meet our French counterparts.

On the 5th [17th] of April, an interesting incident occurred while I was on guard duty. The Cossack pickets captured two men who came out of the city. Half awake, I very lazily interrogated them in German before one of them spoke to me in the most pure Russian and declared himself to be Guard Captain [Alexander Samoylovich] Figner. The name of this partisan, so famous in 1812, was of course very well known to me, but I did not know that he was in Danzig and could not understand how he so calmly departed that city. With respect, I jumped up to scrutinize a man that had made such a historical name, and began to ask him: 'how did you find yourself in Danzig and how did you escape?' But he did not want to waste time with empty questions and asked to be quickly escorted to headquarters. I granted his wish and informed the commander of our detachment about the incident.[60]

On the 12th [24th], the enemy made a strong sortie from Danzig. Against us were sent out several boats with small cannons akin to falconets and an infantry column along the embankment.[61] Compared to the infamous day at the Berezina, this novelty was practically a farce to me. A skirmish counting around 1,500 men with eight guns on both sides was like a cockfight compared to the fire at Polotsk. At first we retreated because the embankment along which the enemy column was marching was to our rear, but when we caught up with them and two guns arrived to reinforce us (while the French had only their small falconets), we did not yield

---

59 Johannisberg was a town outside Geisenheim, Nassau which was renowned for its vineyards and gave its name to a variety of white wine grape. Andreyevskiy et al., *Brockhaus and Efron Dictionary*, s.v. 'Иоганнисберг.'; Wilhelm Hamm, *Das Weinbuch: Der Wein, sein Werden und Wesen* (Leipzig: J. J. Weber, 1874), pp.131-134. [Andreyevskiy et al., *Brockhaus and Efron Dictionary*, s.v. 'Johannisberg.'; Wilhelm Hamm, *The Wine-book: Wine, its Creation and Character* (Leipzig: J. J. Weber, 1874), pp.131-134].

60 Figner infiltrated the city disguised as an Italian, attempted to incite the local population against the French and was captured, but was released for a lack of evidence. Then he worked his way into the staff of General Jean Rapp and was made a courier entrusted with dispatches meant for Napoleon. Naturally upon departing with these letters beyond the French lines, he passed them on to the Russians. Andreyevskiy et al., *Brockhaus and Efron Dictionary*, s.v. 'Фигнер, Александр Самойлович.' [Andreyevskiy et al., *Brockhaus and Efron Dictionary*, s.v. 'Figner, Alexander Samoylovich.']

61 'Falconet' is an anachronism. The lightest guns possibly still in use, unless pulled out of storage from the city's own arsenals, would be the 4-pounder guns of France's Gribeauval system. Robert Wilkinson-Latham, *Napoleon's Artillery* (London: Osprey Publishing, 1975), pp.3-12.

another step despite the numerical superiority of the enemy. The firefight lasted longer than an hour but as our two guns performed far stronger than their trifling things, little by little they turned back the way they had come without breaking into any home where they might profit or make off with livestock. When it came to mounting their boats again, an apparent confusion spread through their ranks. We were ordered to immediately cry '*ura!*' and charge with bayonets. This last manoeuvre completely horrified the enemy and they left two boats behind in their hasty retreat.

We managed to capture several stragglers wading through the water and took them prisoner. Our whole skirmish was over in an hour and a half but off in the distance we heard a heavy cannonade and a firefight and later learned that on the left flank there was a much more earnest sally, which was also a failure for the enemy. We waited all day for a second attack until the evening when we returned to our quarters and discussed with each other the events over dinner. That sally from the French almost seemed like a courteous welcome for the new commander of the besieging corps. By evening, the only one to profit from the day's fighting was Duke Alexander of Württemberg, who took all the glory for repelling the attacks.

On the 15th [27th] of April, they made an attack on Nehrung, which was separated from the main siege corps by the Vistula, over which we had no bridges or vessels to provide reinforcements. The detachment of Colonel Rosen was stationed there, which was 800 men strong and had six guns. The enemy corps that attacked him was 4,000 strong with 16 guns. For two whole hours he withstood the French assault, until finally the impossibility of resisting such a superior force compelled him to retreat for several miles. Our detachment was the closest to the Vistula. We immediately assembled and marched to the bank where we witnessed the defeat of our comrades with an inexpressible anxiety, having no means to help them. We placed all of our six guns on the embankment and began to fire at the other side but quickly saw it was a fruitless effort. Both the enemy and our comrades were out of our range. The main corps sent three strong detachments through Dirschau but it required a detour of 50 *verstas* [53.34 km] and until their arrival, the French spent two whole days in their villages and then returned on the 18th [30th], leaving behind only cats and dogs. Everything else in those homes was stolen and hauled off. Truly, they seized a whole month's forage for the entire city there. Since then, the detachment on that island was reinforced and covered with strong field fortifications, yet from then until late autumn, the French no longer made any motions towards Nehrung.

The Duke of Württemberg took the militia under his special patronage since his arrival at Danzig. He embarked on reorganizing it and soon instead of sixteen undermanned *druzhina*s, it consisted of five consolidated ones. At that time, I was made a company commander, a post that greatly exceeded my rank.

Meanwhile, the besieging corps was reinforced daily by newly arriving forces and it was soon very formidable. On the 28th of May [9th of June], the enemy made

Duke Alexander of Württemberg. Commander of the Russo-Prussian forces at the siege of Danzig. George Dawe, 1825, oil on canvas, St. Petersburg, State Hermitage Museum.

a sortie with all of his garrison and 80 guns in support. The whole day consisted of a very stubborn and heated battle. By evening, the French gave out and returned to their fortresses without breaking through at any one point. Casualties and destruction were immense on both sides, and for what? All the bloodshed was without profit or necessity. Napoleon concluded a truce and on the 29th of May [10th of June], a courier reached us with the news at a time when we were burying our comrades who had just been killed the day before. If that courier had arrived just a day earlier, they would still be alive!

In the last fight, our detachment did not participate much at all. Several boats came to us, as if for our amusement, but they only paddled over, fired and teased us, but did not dare to land on our shore. We responded with vessels of our own and neither side burdened their souls with much sin on that day.

When we learned of the terms of the armistice, we were greatly displeased. We had already driven the French to the point of eating their horses, so it was rumoured, and after their failed sally on the 28th of May, we had hoped to quickly force their surrender. Suddenly it was announced to us that for the whole duration of the armistice we were obligated to provide provisions for the garrison we intended to starve out. It was a grievous blow to us. We did not feel then that in Europe's current political situation, our fortress was of no significance and that

General of Division Jean Rapp, Count Rapp, Commander of the French garrison of Danzig. Cover plate from *Memoirs of General Count Rapp* (London: H. Colburn and Co., 1823).

the armistice signed was in truth Napoleon's greatest mistake which would lead to the Allies marching through the gates of Paris and send the man himself to Elba and St. Helena.

The scenes that unfolded during the truce were very interesting and entertaining. First began a long argument about the quantity of provisions to be provided to the garrison. Rapp wanted enough for 30,000 men but the Duke of Württemberg did not want to relinquish more than 17,000's worth. We received accurate information from the inhabitants of the city and disease had reduced the garrison to 17,000 strong. Rapp protested, lost his patience, and finally conceded. But then upon delivery of the goods something was always missing and the quarrels and complaints were endless.

According to the articles of the armistice, we had to grant each besieged fortress a radius of three *versta*s [3.2 km] to be neutral territory. There from both sides gathered family and friends to say their goodbyes, traders to do business, and curious officers. Among the last were often both we and the French from Danzig. What dramatic events played out there! At the boundary of the neutral zone stood our chain of guards and it was strictly forbidden to admit anyone from the city. But as soon as families were separated and said their goodbyes in various touching displays, the Duke authorized exceptions daily for these unfortunates. Under such conditions, we spent time with the French officers and I will confess that I found their company often quite pleasant. The Duke of Württemberg himself had once met with General Rapp and even the commander of our militia, Senator Bibikov, once dined in the city as a guest. All honorary citizens of Danzig were invited to the feast, and when everyone was seated, a speech was naturally made in honour of the great courage of the defenders, and Rapp said in the most amicable manner: 'So long as Danzig is in our hands, no one shall eat this fat pig!' and pointed at the *Bürgermeister* as he spoke. All the French roared with laughter, but the Russians and Germans met this barb with silence.

At the beginning of the truce, the militia was transferred to the centre of the besieging corps. There we were on high ground and occupied entrenchments on the very most handsome fields by the village of Borgfeld. There, the militia was uniformed in the most dandified fashion, and it was there that our commander, Senator Bibikov, parted with us forever when he left the military service.[62] The truce came to an end on the 14th [28th] of July, but word came from the main army that it was to extend to the 6th [18th] of August. This inactivity eventually became boring. We began to visit the surrounding villages and towns. I found a very pleasant refuge from boredom in Gemlitz, where our baggage train was stationed. There, a new Annchen excited in me the feeling which I feared since my failure in Shlinovo. Fortunately this time, I did not have such drowsiness. On the outskirts of St. Albrecht, a new coffeehouse was founded and officers converged there in crowds. The founder of this institution was an 18-year-old girl who was lively, intelligent, and quite beautiful. Only the colour of her hair was unfavourable, and in the military slang she became nicknamed the 'ginger wench'. This name was not given in contempt, but was simply symptomatic of the army lexicon. Despite her brusque and jesting demeanour, which placed her in the company of many heart-breaking women, she was modest and no one could boast of any sort of intimate conversation with her. Everyone came there to sit, chat, tell jokes, play cards, have a drink, and then leave. For a long time I was speechless among the customers of this beauty until I finally broke into the conversation but even then just as a courtesy. Fate prepared for me a few blows in rapid succession to the most sensitive quarters of my flirtation.

Here was the first. Seeing my shyness and regarding herself safe from my enterprise, the ginger wench (I am truly ashamed to refer to her in that way, but you cannot defy tradition) soon became friendly with me. Everyone noticed this, congratulating me on my victory, and making jokes at my expense. I certainly did not try to convince anyone of my innocence, although I was very confident in it. Gradually I really did become closer to her, so much as my timidity allowed,

---

62 Senator Bibikov left the service on 8 [20] August, 1813 due to failing health and personally handed the militia's banner off to his successor, Major General Vasiliy Vasilyevich Adadurov. Steinheil, *Notes Regarding the St. Petersburg Militia*, Vol. 2, p.91.

but each day I blamed myself for my foolishness, visited the next day and mended everything and then behaved in the very same way. Only when everyone was convinced of my triumph did I see all the signs on her of inclinations toward me, but I kept procrastinating and procrastinating. Finally one evening, my simplicity was too obvious. The weather was rainy and she tried to persuade me to stay for the night. I did not want to seem afraid of the rain and went home, saying that I would stay with her certainly when the weather improved. Alas! The weather never cleared.

On the next day when we came to drink our coffee as usual, we were struck by terrible news. A Tatar colonel I will call Prince B. took our Dulcinea and universal ridicule poured on me from all sides.[63] I joked about it myself and laughed it off, but inside I was furious with myself, with her, and with the whole world.

To find comfort in my grief, I travelled to Gemlitz, where I had not been for some time. What did I find? In the home of my Annchen were officers of the regular army who, not knowing of my domestic ties there, immediately blurted out tales of their successful advances with Annchen playing the starring role. I nearly did not believe those incendiary storytellers and intended to prove the case with experience. I did not wait for that bitter experience however, and left, cursing all levity and love.

All that remained was to seek solace in the heat of battle. The truce ended. The siege resumed in earnest. From February up until that point, it was only a blockade, but now the British brought us siege guns, Congreve rockets, and other paraphernalia. We began to construct fascines and gabions and soon matters came to a boil. On the 17th [29th] of August, magnificent preparations were made for demonstrating the Congreve rockets. An English artillerist deployed his device by the suburb of Ohra and announced to us that 200 rockets would be loosed into the city; that truly 30 locations would be ignited; that we needed to raise a general alarm at this time; that Rapp would become furious and attempt a sally; and that we would repel this attack and follow hot on their heels into the city. The whole corps stood under arms. The barrage began and then ended just as abruptly. Not one section of the city caught fire, Rapp was not furious, there were no sallies and we did not break them – everyone quietly returned to their quarters.

Another scheme was also rather unsuccessful. They began nightly expeditions and attacks on the enemy fortifications on a daily basis. At first, of course, our unexpectedness and superiority in numbers brought us success, but every point that was seized at night typically had to be abandoned again in the morning after, since every field fortification was under the protection of three or four strong

63   Dulcinea del Toboso in Miguel de Cervantes' *Don Quixote* was an imagined personality of immeasurable beauty and grace projected onto an unassuming farm girl, who supposedly had exiled the eponymous character and drove him to grand and equally imaginary adventures to win back her favour. Miguel de Cervantes Saavedra, *Don Quixote de la Mancha*, trans. Charles Jarvis (London: McLean, 1819), pp.9-28.

batteries whose concentrated fire was too devastating. Losing more than a thousand men in this fashion, we finally assumed a common system for sieging and it was truly the best solution. To open the fortifications, the suburbs supporting it needed to be taken. Langfuhr opposite the Olivaer Gate seemed the most convenient point and on the 21st of August [2nd September], our side launched a heavy attack on that borough, while other movements entertained the enemy at other positions. The attack was launched at 4 in the afternoon, a time when we knew Rapp took his dinner. The surprise and speed of the attacks were a complete success. Langfuhr, Strieß, and Neu Schottland were immediately sewn up, but even more painful for Rapp was the destruction of the manor in Schellmühl where his mistress lived. The French rushed at all of our positions furiously to retake them and a fierce battle ensued. The Russian fortitude withstood even the heaviest pressure from the enemy and Rapp only succeeded in securing his favourite manor because it was under the protection of 40 guns from Holm (a heavily fortified island between Danzig and Weichselmünde), whose fire inflicted too many casualties on us to resist. In Langfuhr however, a handful of Poles holed up in two blockhouses desperately resisted all night long, showering their Russian attackers with curses. In the morning, their forts were set on fire and the Poles were all forced out and killed.

On the sea north of Danzig, we also had a considerable force at that time: 80 gunboats, five bomb vessels, two galiotes, one frigate, and 20 transport vessels (which brought us the siege guns). We decided to bring our significant naval power into action. On the 23rd of August [5th of September], we deployed the whole flotilla against Westerplatte and Fahrwasser. From 10 in the morning a most terrible cannonade opened up from every ship, seeking to destroy every coastal fortification, and a landing party was prepared on our transports for occupying those fortresses. By evening, the ships moved to Putzig for repairs. The misfortune of this attempt could be attributed completely to strange and unforeseen reasons. It had to be attempted again. The boats could be repaired in five days and the shore party (among which was our *druzhina*) was left aboard the ships to accustom the men to the sea. But our terrestrial nature did not agree with the sea and the fate prepared for us was an altogether unexpected grief.

On the night of the 23rd and 24th [5th and 6th of September], a storm hit and we could not dock on the shore, so we began to manoeuvre every which way over the Baltic Sea. My skipper was an Englishman who was immensely fond of me because when I first met him I spoke a few words of English – that was the weakest chord to pluck in an English heart. If he is forced to speak any other language, his treatment will always be cold, but a few English words (à la Figaro) and he melted.[64]

64 In Pierre Beaumarchais's *The Marriage of Figaro*, the eponymous character claims that one can negotiate any number of social situations in English by simply exclaiming 'goddamn!' and although it may be dressed up with 'a few other words' before and after, 'goddamn' is the basis of the whole language.

The landing party on the whole became seasick and by morning they all lay on the deck in the most wretched throws of agony. My captain fruitlessly worried over me but I did not drink any rum, lemon was no help, and even so much as looking at food made me vomit. I did not know anything more excruciating than that malady. Anguished and disgusted by everything, I was weakened by constant hunger, thirst and vomiting. We spent three days in that sorry situation but the wind finally died down, the sea calmed and we could again see our coveted shore. The commander-in-chief was immediately informed that the whole landing party was laid up without their sea legs and each soldier needed two men to stand him up. It was decided to land the infantry on the shore at Koliebke and let them rest until further orders. Somehow we piled into the boats and were promptly dumped onto the beach. We lay on the bank for a good two hours without having the strength to get up. Everything spun around us: the sea, the ships, and the village. With the assistance of the good villagers, we were moved onto wagons, but we clung on dearly for fear of falling out, as still the horses, houses, and pedestrians, everything waltzed around us in the most fantastic manner. We took shelter under a hut, which also danced. We sat at the dinner table and it spun. We climbed into our beds and they jumped. Finally we fell asleep and in our dreams everything was tumbling. It was unbearable. We had at least the whole day to sleep soundly, and the first desire upon waking was 'food!' I think the Prussian peasants were amazed by our northern appetite like it was some sort of insatiability. As soon as we had our fill, we went to sleep again, as many began to complain they were dizzy again after lunch.

Thus we lived until the 3rd [15th] of September. On that day, we again boarded the boats and were taken to our previous transports. My Englishman was extraordinarily delighted to see me again and bombarded me with English phrases, only a tenth of which I could only understand. I only answered 'yes' very drowsily. During dinner we came to understand each other better and in the morning at breakfast, I made frequent use of the Figaro's 'goddamn!'

This new attack began at 9 in the morning. Only Russian soldiers could do such things as what we witnessed. We ourselves stood at a very respectable distance, having before us in the second line the bomb vessels, galiotes, and frigate, while the first line was entirely comprised of gunboats. The enemy saw our antics from afar and had prepared for us an excellent reception. As soon as the ships arrived, the enemy unleashed a cannonade on us from more than a hundred guns loaded with solid shot, but they silently rowed forward and did not respond to the fire. They all rowed for more than 200 *sazhen*s [426.72 m] under such fire and then the enemy switched to canister, and still they rowed under the terrible hale of canister balls without returning a single shot. Finally, at half the distance of canister range,

Pierre Beaumarchais, *La Folle Journée ou Le Mariage de Figaro* (Paris: Ruault, 1785), pp.69-70. [Pierre Beaumarchais, *The Folly of the Day or The Marriage of Figaro* (Paris: Ruault, 1785), pp.69-70].

we stopped, lined up, shouted '*ura!*' and opened from every ship the most terrible barrage, reinforced from behind by the bomb vessels. It was a beautiful sight, especially for those of us in the third line! Many had already seen dangers, many had heard cannonades, many had seen examples of fearlessness – but this gunfire stunned us, and the courage of these sailors was amazing.

I also saw for the first time the use of heated shot, which the French fired at our fleet from the shore. One such ball struck the powder magazine on a gun boat and the explosion sent fifty brave sailors high into the air. One officer managed to evade fate, since the commander of his vessel had sent him to the rear admiral to report that the boat was badly damaged and could no longer remain in the line. After receiving permission to withdraw her, he was already making the return trip to his vessel when his comrades were blown up. Surviving their fate, he would only meet another immediately after: he rowed his skiff to the vessel of the divisional commander and, just after climbing aboard, he was mortally wounded by grapeshot.

Mutual exchanges of fire continued until 6 in the evening, but not one of the enemy's batteries were knocked out while twelve of our boats were nearly torn to pieces and more than 300 men had fallen out of our line – so the attack ended. No one could have shown more bravery or self-sacrifice, yet success was impossible. After the prior three-day storm and during the fresh breezes of that day, the sea was rolling hefty waves. How could a ship in such motion aim its cannons true and penetrate the embrasures of a coastal battery?

After that unsuccessful expedition, one more scheme had to be attempted. A Prussian engineer of the previous siege announced that the weakest point of the fortress was situated on the flooded plains, which was exactly true. He explained that in the autumn the Vistula ebbed very low but the even lower fields were flooded in the spring, and it was true! He proposed, consequently, to dig a rampart on the Vistula and after the water flooded, to begin an attack from the other side. We immediately set to work. The dike was built and the water really began to drain from the fields, the sight of which moved me tremendously. What ecstasy! But fate was not done toying with us. During that night, a strong wind blew in off the sea and the Vistula swelled and rose, and instead of the flooding covering some 15 *verstas* [16 km], it stretched as far as 30 [32 km] by the next day. Many livestock drowned and huts were washed away immediately, but the residents all managed to escape and were very cross about the clever scheming of their fellow countryman.

All that remained was to conduct a regular siege, and from then on the affair went smoothly. Assembling all the siege guns, a cannonade was opened up across the city on the 7th [19th] of October. In less than half an hour, Danzig was already burning in four places. The shots were directed at the lit places and we could see from the heights through our telescopes as the flames flowed from house to house, from street to street; as the residents ran and bustled around trying to save their property; as fire engines and portions of the garrison fought back the flames; and as our batteries continued to operate without interruption, striking those crowds and forcing them to disperse, letting everyone fall victim to cruel fate. That brutal fire raged for three days and thousands of families were left without food or shelter, but the disaster had only just begun.

In order to get rid of those poor people, Rapp announced that he agreed to release them from the city. The unfortunates fell for his deception. With delight, they hastened to take advantage of Rapp's permission and crowds rushed out of the city, past the French forward chain, and then what? From the Russian chain they were met with gunshots! A few determined people went as representatives to the commander of the chain, who also came out to meet with them and announced to them that he was under strict orders: none of the residents could be permitted to cross the chain and that if anyone tried to sneak through the posts or rush past them in desperation, they would be shot. With all the melancholy of death, they turned back toward the French chain, but, if you can imagine the horror, those posts also greeted them with gunfire and threats. What could these poor souls do? They were left in the open air between two warring forces, under fire from both sides, without food or hope of salvation. It is impossible to describe the suffering of those émigrés. Many women had come out of the city while pregnant and the horror and despair hastened their labour. In that position without charity or shelter, on the bare ground in the October night, with cannonballs whistling overhead as the guns thundered on the horizon, risking death by starvation – even now their tears and cries for help shred a soldier's heart. The commander of the chain sent a report to the Duke of Württemberg describing the image he saw and asked permission to admit the crowd past his line. The law of war was pitiless. A new strict prohibition followed. The refugees lived for more than a week on roots, herbs, and small rations secretly passed to them at night by compassionate soldiers. Gradually the crowd began to thin out and then it disappeared. Their bodies were buried where they fell, yet it turned out that 460 people left the city and only 112 bodies were found. What became of the remainder? Naturally, no one was looking for them but each knew that, for the honour of humanity, soldiers and officers standing watch had admitted them at night and donated to them the means of life whenever an opportunity to violate the order presented itself.

After the daily cannonades, fires, and mutual attacks, the first parallel was finally dug opposite Jesuiterschanze. Then a new kind of service began for us: trench watch. It must be said that this kind was rather unpleasant. To sit in a pit for the whole day, constantly being showered with those damned potatoes (as we called canister), watching all night for falling asterisks (as we called bombs) and throwing ourselves flat on the ground when they fell (and this was the most safe method against bursting bombs, since they exploded upward in a wide cone), and all the while, as usual, we were starving. Such was all the joy of trench warfare!

It was interesting how things by habit ceased to be frightening. Young Prussian sutlers and canteen girls came to our camp every day throughout the whole siege, bringing bread, vodka, cherries, and spiced confectionaries. Since our trenches were first dug, we were gradually advancing and the dangers increased with proximity, but with the same punctuality they found us every morning, crouching slightly as shot whistled overhead and telling jokes while the iron potatoes showered the earth around us. With good cheer they told us the latest news and did not depart until their entire stock was depleted. The village boys often amused us with their daring. Not letting the enemy's shots go to waste, they pulled them out of the ground and, depending on the calibre, distributed them across our batteries so we could return-ship them to their home addresses. For each recovered ball they were paid a *Groschen* (approximately seven kopecks), and this labour usually involved the boys from the neighbouring villages. It was quite a sight to see them all standing impatiently under fire waiting for the balls to land. As soon as one slammed into the earth, they immediately ran over and pried it out. We shouted at them in vain to wait a little, because many of the shots were hollowed balls filled with charges that would explode and kill with their fragments, but it never stopped the young boys. They wanted to quickly earn their coin and buy themselves something sweet.

On the 24th of October [5th of November], the French tried another unsuccessful attack on Nehrung where they had been successful on the 15th [27th] of April. Ever since, the enemy never troubled the detachment there. It is not surprising that such inactivity gave birth to carelessness. Indeed they had so cleverly crept up on the positions that they caught the commander of the detachment in a deep slumber and barely gave him time to escape. But in this case, not only did they find no provisions to haul away, but were repelled with losses by a reserve force half an hour later.

Either in response to that incident or by some other directive, our *druzhina* was ordered to relocate to Nehrung and reinforce the detachment there. The route there still ran through the town of Dirschau and we slogged our way there through the thickest mud over a period of four days. When we arrived and stayed for three days, a terrible boredom fell over us. After the most active conditions full of danger at every moment, we were suddenly relocated to a land frozen in perfect stasis. There was only lethargic anxiety. We spread out seeking excitement. With the head of the 1st Company, several of us took our leave in the town of Elbing, which lies about 60 *verstas* [64 km] from Danzig. The pretext of this leave was to exchange the company's money. The colonel granted us five days.

We slogged through the unyielding mud for three days and that alone did not leave enough time to turn back and report for duty when we were due, but since the blame for the delay was constant and already established, we decided to stay longer all the same. Could we have decided any differently? A beautiful town, an exceptional community, a marvellous reception wherever we went, with money to spend, our youth and a willingness to fall in love… day after day, joy after joy, pleasure after pleasure. We stayed there for three weeks. My comrade fell in love with the daughter of one of the municipal counsellors. They were a match. He came from a good family, held a decent rank (he was a twenty-year-old collegiate assessor), was well educated, could play the fortepiano beautifully, had a most noble-hearted spirit and was very handsome. Was it any wonder that the Germans took to him so well? Their hands were all over him, and I was invited to tag along. Beside him, all of my natural talents evaporated, but I did not envy him. I was busy with very modest flirtations. I was passionately in love with the daughter of the host of our English inn and was driven crazy by her. One of the daily visitors there, a merchant, because my friend and solicitor. He seemed to sincerely want to help us, but Theresa, yielding to the power of my love, wanted to legally be married and it kept a tight rein on my outbursts of romance. Regardless, every day I was more and more inflamed, and the desire for intimacy burned my young blood. My German friend worried over me cordially and I took the opportunity to give him instructions for a mission. I suddenly discovered that he was in love with Theresa as well and had once offered her his hand in marriage but was rejected. I exploded! I rushed toward him and told him what I had learned and he confessed to it all being true, but half-heartedly. 'Why are you angry?' he asked. 'There are maybe ten men in love with Theresa. Does that prevent her from preferring you? If you marry her, she will surely be happy, and I, loving her, will be very happy for her. You do not really want to seduce her'. I immediately relented and apologized. His selflessness touched me. I also decided to sacrifice and instructed him to tell her father that I truly intended to marry her. He immediately fulfilled my task. Theresa was delighted and her father was amazed, but hoped however to amaze me. He instructed that I be told that no matter how great the honour done to his daughter, he would give her 20,000 thalers and that any groom would be worthy of it. Both he and Theresa expressed their total consent. I was overjoyed, flew to him, hugged everyone and from that moment I enjoyed all the rights of the groom.

My officer companion needed to be told everything and that was my greatest fear. Somehow I hinted to him about my love and it did not surprise him, but when I elaborated on my intention to marry Theresa, he presented to me all the follies of this act. I ceased arguing the point when word came from Danzig that Rapp had concluded the capitulation of the city and consequently we had to hurry back for a victorious procession.[65] I expected it, but at the same time I knew that my marriage could not now be performed and was postponed. I was sure to myself that it would be concluded later. The next morning, I announced to Theresa that I was riding to Danzig the day after to arrange my own affairs and I would return as soon as possible. She cried and I kissed her and reassured her. After one of the happiest days of my life, I was gone in the next morning.

In a sad mood, both I and my comrade departed. He was leaving his beloved and was loved, but for him there was no other measure of success besides cold

---

65 Rapp signed the terms of surrender of 17 [29] December, 1813, and the garrison surrendered to the Allies on the 1 [13] January, 1814 to afford Rapp the prestige of having defended the city for a full year. Steinheil, *Notes Regarding the St. Petersburg Militia*, Vol. 2, pp.132-133.

Hymenaios.[66] He had enough strength to break away from that outcome. A few miles from Elbing was a common crossing over the Vistula (or its branch, the Nogat) and when we reached it, we were suddenly told that heavy ice flowing down the river had ceased all traffic and that it would take at least two weeks to get across. What could be done to counter fate? We were privately glad to be turning back to Elbing and appeared before the commandant. He already knew about the delay from the cessation of communications and gave us new passes for quartering. At once, we were again with our yearning beauties. Those two weeks passed quickly and despite all of our joy, we were very annoyed that the whole affair at Danzig ended without us. The Elbing newspapers informed us about the Emperor's disapproval of the capitulation; about his order to issue an ultimatum to the garrison that they either surrender to become prisoners of war or to continue defending; about their acceptance of the Sovereign's will; about the ceremonial surrender of the fortress and city; about the departure of the forces within and the festivities held in Danzig in honour of the Russians – all of it happening without us! We inquired about the ferry to cross the river every day and would depart at the first opportunity.

It did not benefit us much to return guilty. Our return was too delayed to be overlooked. I, as the junior officer, had the excuse of being required to listen to my senior comrade. He did not know how to excuse himself before our colonel, but it all ended in the most merciful fashion. We travelled to Danzig to walk about and see its sights.

It was a great joy to pass over the trenches and batteries and no longer hear the perpetual accompaniment of solid shot and canister fire. To ride into the city that had nearly held us away at a fearful distance for a full year, to walk along its broken streets and past its ruined buildings, to repeat to yourself that you were victorious; all of these were our joys. But these vain feelings were soon fulfilled, dulled, and became tired. A man craves pleasure and then he is bored of it. Despite the public displays of rapture, everywhere was visible poverty and even dishonesty. The benefits of Napoleon's rule had spoiled the citizens of Danzig and they did not want to return to the Kingdom of Prussia. They even sent a deputation to Alexander asking to be taken under his possession but among the Allied monarchs the issue was already settled. The deputies were told that it was not their prerogative to choose who ruled them and that they were to appear before their rightful sovereign, the King of Prussia.

So ended the siege of Danzig. From the day the trenches were dug, that terrible fortress was forced to surrender in less than two months. The action of the Russian artillery surpassed all praise. The seven years of labour poured into the

---

66   Hymen or Hymenaios was the Greek god of marriage, son of Apollo and one of the muses. Andreyevskiy et al., *Brockhaus and Efron Dictionary*, s.v. 'Гименей.' [Andreyevskiy et al., *Brockhaus and Efron Dictionary*, s.v. 'Hymen.']

fortifications by those French engineers were so beaten by our shot that communications even between their batteries were hindered by the wreckage. Nearly all of their guns were knocked out and our most advanced trenches cut into the glacis. The present art of war has no more use for insurmountable fortresses when you need only dig trenches before them.

The capture of Danzig was shortly after followed by a Supreme Decree from His Majesty on the disbandment of the militia. Almost none of us were content with it. Allied forces then marched into France. The last act of that grand drama had begun: the Fall of Napoleon, but we were ordered to leave the stage. It was terrible! Our soldiers had their muskets confiscated, being useless items for a peaceful villager, and were sent home. We hated to watch it unfold. So many memories for a warrior were tied to his weapon, his witness and comrade in those battles of two years! It would have been for him and his children a relic, which his grandchildren would come to admire and tell tales of that great and trying era.

What else is there to say about our service? The returning march was nothing but the stroll of idle men.[67] In Königsberg, we learned of the capture of Paris and the end of the war. Rejoicing in the greatness and glory of the Russian arms, we were sad however that we could not participate in that momentous achievement which began a new epoch in the history of nations, which again changed the geography of Europe, which overthrew a dynasty that had reigned for ten years, and which elevated Russia to an unprecedented degree of power, glory, and majesty.

On the 12th [24th] of June, we returned to Saint Petersburg. Greeted by the Empress Dowager [Maria Feodorovna], the Duke of Württemberg, and the Minister of War Gorchakov, we assembled on St. Isaac's Square, the same place we stood when we received our banner in 1812, and were proud to be able to say that no shame came to those colours. The same reverend bishop now blessed our return as had originally bestowed on us our colours and its cross when we first departed the city. What a great change had occurred since then! From such a struggle, Russia emerged victorious!

Those of us remaining who affected that upheaval were not great. Out of 14,000 warriors who stood in our ranks then, now only 4,000 remained. Where did they all go? To those who died with honour for your country: peace be with you!

That was how we began, fulfilled, and ended our service. In those great events, we will soon be forgotten. It is the fate of all human affairs. We dissolved and went our separate ways, and I can boast the latest folly: returning to my old department in the civil service instead of transferring into the military. Even now I regret it! Should even very little occur in my career, it would be enough! But the future is in the hands of the Almighty. Amen.

---

67 Zotov's note: 'For the curious: What of Theresa and the wedding? Forgive me, Lord! I could not marry her. Our good colonel talked me out of it and Theresa married the very merchant who had been my solicitor.'

Bibliography

Complete Collection of Laws of the Russian Empire (Moscow: II Department of His Imperial Majesty's Own Chancellery, 1830). [*Полное Собрание Законов Российской Империи* (Moscow: II Отделение Собственное Его Императорского Величества Канцелярии, 1830).]

His Imperial Majesty's Military Regulations on the Field Cavalry Service (St. Petersburg: State Military Collegium, 1797). [*Его Императорского Величества Воинский Устав о Полевой Кавалерийской Службе* (St. Petersburg: Государственная Военная Коллегия, 1797).]

List of Russian Military Vessels from 1668 to 1860 (St. Petersburg: Press of the Naval Ministry, 1872). [*Список Русских Военных Судов с 1668 по 1860 год* (St. Petersburg: Типография Морского Министерва, 1872).]

Menologium with a List of Ranking Individuals or a General State of the Russian Empire in the Year of Our Lord 1812 (St. Petersburg: Imperial Academy of Sciences, 1812). [*Месяцеслов с Росписью Чиновных Особ, или Общий Штат Российской Империи на Лето от Рождества Христова 1812* (St. Petersburg: Императорская Академия Наук, 1812).]

Military Regulations on the Infantry Service (St. Petersburg: Press of the Scientific Committee of the Artillery Department, 1811). [*Воинской Устав о Пехотной Службе* (St. Petersburg: Типография Ученого Комитета по Артиллерийской Части, 1811).]

Saint Petersburg Pocket Menologium for the Year of Our Lord 1813 (St. Petersburg: Imperial Academy of Sciences, 1813). [*Санктпетербургский Карманный Месяцеслов на лето от Рождества Христова 1813* (St. Petersburg: Императорская Академия Наук, 1813).]

Saint Petersburg Pocket Menologium for the Year of Our Lord 1814 (St. Petersburg: Imperial Academy of Sciences, 1814). [*Санктпетербургский Карманный Месяцеслов на лето от Рождества Христова 1814* (St. Petersburg: Императорская Академия Наук, 1814).]

Aller, Samuil, *Description of the Flooding formerly in St. Petersburg on the 7th November 1824* (St. Petersburg: Press of the Department of Public Education, 1826). [Аллер, Самуил, *Описание Наводнения, бывшего в Санкт-Петербурге 7 числа ноября 1824 года* (St. Petersburg: Типография Департамента Народного Просвещения, 1826).]

Andreyevskiy, I. E., K. K. Arsen'yev and F. F. Petrushevskiy (eds.), *Brockhaus and Efron Encyclopedic Dictionary* (St. Petersburg: Efron, 1890). [Андреевский, И. Е., К. К. Арсеньев and Ф. Ф. Петрушевский (eds.), *Энциклопедический Словарь Брокгауза и Ефрона* (St. Petersburg: Ефрон, 1890).]

Anon., *Pocket Postal Atlas of the Russian Empire* (St. Petersburg: His Imperial Majesty's Map Depot, 1808). [*Карманный Почтовый Атлас Российской Империи* (St. Petersburg: Депо Карт Его Императорского Величества, 1808).]

Beaumarchais, Pierre, *The Folly of the Day or The Marriage of Figaro* (Paris: Ruault, 1785). [Beaumarchais, Pierre, *La Folle Journée ou Le Mariage de Figaro* (Paris: Ruault, 1785).]

Bednyy, Demyan (ed.), *The Complete Collection of Works by Ivan Krylov* (Moscow: State Publishing House of Fictional Literature, 1946). [Бедный, Демьян (ed.), *Полное Собрание Сочинений Ивана Крылова* (Moscow: Государственное Издательство Художественной Литературы, 1946).]

Beskrovnyy, Lyubomir (ed.), *M. I. Kutuzov: Collection of Documents* (Moscow: Military Publishing of the Ministry of Defense of the USSR, 1954). [Бескровный, Любомир (ed.), *М. И. Кутузов: Сборник Документов* (Moscow: Военное Издательство Министерства Обороны СССР, 1954).]

Bezotosnyy, Viktor (ed.), *The 'Patriotic War of 1812' Encyclopedia*, (Moscow: Russian Political Encyclopedia, 2004). [Безотосный, Виктор (ed.), *Энциклопедия 'Отечественная Война 1812 года'* (Moscow: Российская Политическая Энциклопедия, 2004).]

Bobrovskiy, Pavel, *History of the Leib-Guard Uhlan Regiment of Her Majesty Alexandra Feodorovna* (St. Petersburg: Expedition for Storing State Papers, 1903). [Бобровский, Павел, *История Лейб-Гвардии Уланского Ея Величества Александры Феодоровны Полка* (St. Petersburg: Экспедиция Заготовления Государственных Бумаг, 1903).]

Bogdanovich, Modest, *History of the Patriotic War of 1812* (St. Petersburg: Firm of Strugovshchik, Pokhitonov, Vodov and Co., 1860). [Богданович, Модест, *История Отечественной Войны 1812 года* (St. Petersburg: Торговый дом Струговщика, Похитонова, Водова и Ко., 1860).]

Bogdanovich, Modest, *History of the War of 1813 for the Independence of Germany* (St. Petersburg: Press of the Staff of Military Educational Institutions, 1863). [Богданович, Модест, *История Войны 1813 года за Независимость Германии* (St. Petersburg: Типография Штаба Военно-Учебных Заведений, 1863).]

Du Camp, Jules, *History of the Army and all its Regiments* (Paris: A. Barbier, 1850). [Du Camp, Jules, *Histoire de l'Armée et de tout les Régiments* (Paris: A. Barbier, 1850).]

Cardarelli, François (Trans. M. J. Shields), *Encyclopedia of Scientific Units, Weights and Measures* (London: Springer, 2004).

Cervantes Saavedra, Miguel de (Trans. Charles Jarvis), *Don Quixote de la Mancha* (London: McLean, 1819).

Chambray, Georges de, *History of the Russian Expedition* (Paris: Pillet, 1825). [Chambray, Georges de, *Histoire de l'Expédition de Russie* (Paris: Pillet, 1825).]

Dolgov, S. and A. Afanas'yev (eds.), *History of the Leib-Guard Preobrazhenskiy Regiment, 1683-1883* (St. Petersburg: Press of I. N. Skorokhodov, 1888). [Долгов, С. and А. Афанасьев (eds.), *История Лейб-Гвардии Преображенского полка, 1683-1883* (St. Petersburg: Типография И. Н. Скороходова, 1888).]

Ebers, John (ed.), *The New and Complete Dictionary of the German and English Languages* (Leipzig: Britkopf and Haertel, 1799).

Friedrich Wilhelm III, 'To My People.' *The Silesian Privileged Newspaper*, 20 March, 1813. [Friedrich Wilhelm III. 'An Mein Volk.' *Schlesische Privilegirte Zeitung*, 20 March, 1813.]

Georgiyevskiy, Mikhail (ed.), *Russo-Karelian Dictionary* (St. Petersburg: V. D. Smirnov Press, 1908). [Георгиевский, Михаил ed. *Русско-Карельский Словарь* (St. Petersburg: Типография В. Д. Смирнова, 1908).]

Griboyedov, Alexandr, *Woe from Wit* (St. Petersburg: Press of P. A. Kulish, 1862). [Грибоедов, Александр, *Горе от Ума* (St Petersburg: Типография П А. Кулиша, 1862).]

Gulevich, Sergey. *History of the Leib-Guard Finland Regiment* (St. Petersburg: Economical Typo-Lithography, 1906). [Гулевич, Сергей. *История Лейб-Гвардии Финляндского Полка* (St. Petersburg: Экономическая Типо-Литография, 1906).]

Hamm, Wilhelm, *The Wine Book: Wine, its Creation and Character* (Leipzig: J. J. Weber, 1874). [Hamm, Wilhelm, *Das Weinbuch: Der Wein, sein Werden und Wesen* (Leipzig: J. J. Weber, 1874).]

Haydn, Joseph, *The Book of Dignities Containing the Rolls of the Official Personages of the British Empire* (London: Long, Brown, Green and Longmans, 1851).

Hosking, Geoffrey, *Russia: People and Empire* (Cambridge: Harvard University Press, 1997).

Lüdinghausen genannt Wolff, Otto von, *History of the Royal Prussian 2nd Garde-Regiment of Foot, 1813-1882* (Berlin: E. S. Mittler und Sonn, 1882). [Lüdinghausen genannt Wolff, Otto von, *Geschichte des Königlich Preußischen 2. Garde-Regiments zu Fuß, 1813-1882* (Berlin: E. S. Mittler und Sonn, 1882).]

Manring, M. M., Alan Hawk, Jason Calhoun and Romney Andersen, 'Treatment of Wounds: A Historical Review.' *The National Center for Biotechnology Information*, last modified 2009. https://www.ncbi.nlm.nih.gov/pmc/articles/PMC2706344/

Mikhaylovskiy-Danilevskiy, Aleksandr, *Description of the Campaign in France in 1814* (St Petersburg: Press of the Department of Foreign Trade, 1836). [Михайловский-Данилевский, Александр. *Описание Похода во Францию в 1814 году* (St. Petersburg: Типография Департамента Внешней Торговли, 1836).]

Mikhaylovskiy-Danilevskiy, Aleksandr, *Description of the Second War between Emperor Alexander and Napoleon in the Years 1806 and 1807* (St Petersburg: Staff of the Independent Corps of the Interior Guard, 1846). [Михайловский-Данилевский, Александр. *Описание Второй Войны Императора Александра с Наполеоном в 1806 и 1807 годах* (St. Petersburg: Штаб Отдельного Корпуса Внутренней Стражи, 1846).]

Nazarov, Pamfil (ed. V. I. Lestvitsyn), 'Memoirs of the Soldier Pamfil Nazarov, the Future Monk Metrophanes', *Russian Antiquity*. Vol. 22, pp.529-556. [Назаров, Памфил, (В. И. Лествицын ed.), 'Записки Солдата Памфила Назарова в Иночестве Митрофана.' In *Русская Старина*. Vol. 22, pp.529-556.]

Ostroukhov, Ivan. 'Recollections of Ivan Menshoy', *Russian Antiquity*. Vol. 10, pp. 46-59. [Остроухов, Иван. 'Воспоминания Ивана Меньшого.' In *Русская Старина*. Vol. 10, pp.46-59.]

Palmer, George (trans.), *The Odyssey of Homer* (Cambridge: Riverside Press, 1892).

Popovitskiy, E. A. (ed.), *The Complete Orthodox Theological Encyclopedic Dictionary* (St. Petersburg: P. P. Soykin, 1912). [Поповицкий, Е. А. (ed.), *Полный Православный Богословский Энциклопедический Словарь* (St. Petersburg: П. П. Сойкин, 1912).]

Pushkarev, Ivan, *Description of St. Petersburg and the County Capitals of the St. Petersburg Governorate* (St. Petetersburg: Press of N. Grech, 1839). [Пушкарев, Иван, *Описание Санктпетербурга и Уездных Городов С. Петербургской Губернии* (St. Petersburg: Типография Н. Греча), 1839.]

Samokhvalov, N. F. (ed.), *Governorates of the Russian Empire* (Moscow: Russian Ministry of Internal Affairs, 2003). [Самохвалов, Н. Ф. (ed.), *Губернии Российской Империи* (Moscow: Russian Ministry of Internal Affairs, 2003).]

Seleshnikov, Semyon, *History of Calendars and Chronology* (Moscow: Science, 1790). [Селешников, Семен, *История календаря и хронология* (Moscow: Наука, 1970).]

Shepelyov, Leonid, *Titles, Uniforms and Orders of the Russian Empire* (Moscow: Tsentrpoligraf, 2005). [Шепелёв, Леонид. *Титулы, Мундиры и Ордена Российской Империи* (Moscow: Центрполиграф, 2005).]

Skalon, D. A. (ed.), *Centenary of the War Ministry 1802-1902* (St. Petersburg: Press of P. F. Panteleyev and 'Prudence' Press, 1902). [Скалон, Д. А. ed. *Столетие Военного Министерства 1802-1902* (St. Petersburg: Типография П. Ф. Пантелеева and «Бережливость», 1902).]

Steinheil, Vladimir, *Notes Regarding the Creation and Campaigning of the St. Petersburg Militia against the Enemies of the Fatherland in 1812 and 1813* (St. Petersburg: Press of V. Plavil'shchikov, 1814). [Штейнгейль, Владимир, *Записки Касательно Составления и Самого Похода Санктпетербургского Ополчения против Врагов Отечества в 1812 и 1813 годах* (St. Petersburg: Типография В. Плавильщикова, 1814).]

Valville, Alexandre, *Treatise on the Counterpoint* (St. Petersburg: Press of Karl Kray, 1817). [Valville, Alexandre, *Traité sur la Contre-Pointe* (St. Petersburg: Типография Карла Краия, 1817).

Venables, Richard Lister, *Domestic Scenes in Russia* (London: John Murray, 1856).

Viskovatov, Alexandr, *Historical Description of the Dress and Armament of the Russian Army* (St. Petersburg: Military Press, 1860). [Висковатов, Александр, *Историческое Описание Одежды и Вооружения Российских Войск* (St. Petersburg: Военная Типография, 1860).]

Ward, A. W., G. W. Prothero and Stanley Leathes (eds.) *Cambridge Modern History* (Cambridge: University Press, 1906).

Wilkinson-Latham, Robert, *Napoleon's Artillery* (London: Osprey Publishing, 1975).

Zhmodikov, Alexander and Yuriy Zhmodikov, *Tactics of the Russian Army in the Napoleonic Wars* (West Chester, Ohio: Nafziger Collection, 2003).

Zotov, Rafail, *Stories of the Campaigns of 1812 and 1813 from an Ensign of the Saint-Petersburg Militia* (St. Petersburg: Press of I. Glazunov, A. Smirdin & Co., 1836). [Зотов, Рафаил, *Рассказы о Походах 1812-го и 1813-го годов, Прапорщика Санктпетербургскаго Ополчения* (St. Petersburg: Типография И. Глазунова, А. Смирдина, и ко., 1836).]

Index

From Reason to Revolution series – Warfare 1721-1815

http://www.helion.co.uk/published-by-helion/reason-to-revolution-1721-1815.html

The 'From Reason to Revolution' series covers the period of military history c. 1721–1815, an era in which fortress-based strategy and linear battles gave way to the nation-in-arms and the beginnings of total war.

This era saw the evolution and growth of light troops of all arms, and of increasingly flexible command systems to cope with the growing armies fielded by nations able to mobilise far greater proportions of their manpower than ever before. Many of these developments were fired by the great political upheavals of the era, with revolutions in America and France bringing about social change which in turn fed back into the military sphere as whole nations readied themselves for war. Only in the closing years of the period, as the reactionary powers began to regain the upper hand, did a military synthesis of the best of the old and the new become possible.

The series will examine the military and naval history of the period in a greater degree of detail than has hitherto been attempted, and has a very wide brief, with the intention of covering all aspects from the battles, campaigns, logistics, and tactics, to the personalities, armies, uniforms, and equipment.

Submissions

The publishers would be pleased to receive submissions for this series. Please contact series editor Andrew Bamford via email (andrewbamford18@gmail.com), or in writing to Helion & Company Limited, 26 Willow Road, Solihull, West Midlands, B91 1UE.

Titles

No.1 *Lobositz to Leuthen. Horace St Paul and the Campaigns of the Austrian Army in the Seven Years War 1756-57* Translated with additional materials by Neil Cogswell (IBN 978-1-911096-67-2)

No 2 *Glories to Useless Heroism. The Seven Years War in North America from the French journals of Comte Maurés de Malartic, 1755-1760* William Raffle (ISBN 978-1-1911512-19-6) (paperback)

No 3 *Reminiscences 1808-1815 Under Wellington. The Peninsular and Waterloo Memoirs of William Hay* William Hay, with notes and commentary by Andrew Bamford (ISBN 978-1-1911512-32-5)

No 4 *Far Distant Ships. The Royal Navy and the Blockade of Brest 1793-1815* Quintin Barry (ISBN 978-1-1911512-14-1)

No 5 *Godoy's Army. Spanish Regiments and Uniforms from the Estado Militar of 1800* Charles Esdaile and Alan Perry (ISBN 978-1-911512-65-3) (paperback)

No 6 *On Gladsmuir Shall the Battle Be! The Battle of Prestonpans 1745* Arran Johnston (ISBN 978-1-911512-83-7)

No 7 *The French Army of the Orient 1798-1801. Napoleon's Beloved 'Egyptians'* Yves Martin (ISBN 978-1-911512-71-4)*

No 8 *The Autobiography, or Narrative of a Soldier. The Peninsular War Memoirs of William Brown of the 45th Foot* William Brown, with notes and commentary by Steve Brown (ISBN 978-1-911512-94-3) (paperback)

No 9 *Recollections from the Ranks. Three Russian Soldiers' Autobiographies from the Napoleonic Wars* Translated and annotated by Darrin Boland (ISBN 978-1-912174-18-8) (paperback)

Books within this series are published in two major formats. 'Falconets' are paperbacks, page size 248mm × 180 mm, with high visual content including colour plates; 'Culverins' are hardback monographs, page size 234mm × 156mm. Books marked * in the list above are Falconets, all others are Culverins unless otherwise noted.

Milton Keynes UK
Ingram Content Group UK Ltd.
UKHW050147201123
432895UK00010B/66